PEOPLE OF THE BOOK?

Books by John Barton

People of the Book?
The Authority of the Bible in Christianity

Reading the Old Testament:
Method in Biblical Study

John Barton

PEOPLE OF THE BOOK?

The Authority of the Bible in Christianity

———

Westminster/John Knox Press
Louisville, Kentucky

First published in Great Britain 1988
SPCK, Holy Trinity Church, Marylebone Road, London NW1 4DU

Copyright © John Barton 1988

First American edition

Published by Westminster/John Knox Press
Louisville, Kentucky

PRINTED IN THE UNITED STATES OF AMERICA
9 8 7 6 5 4 3 2 1

Library of Congress Cataloging-in-Publication Data

Barton, John, 1948–
  People of the book?

  Bibliography: p.
  Includes index.
  1. Bible—Criticism, interpretation, etc. 2. Bible—
Evidences, authority, etc. I. Title.
BS511.2.B39 1988   220.6   88-28047
ISBN 0-664-25066-1

For Mary and Katie

Contents

	Foreword	ix
1.	The Bible in the Christian Faith	1
2.	Prophecy and Fulfilment	12
3.	The Question of the Canon	24
4.	The Bible as Evidence	36
5.	The Bible as Theology	48
6.	Salvation by Hermeneutics	59
7.	The Bible in Liturgy	70
8.	The Word of God and the Words of Men	80
	Select Bibliography	91
	Index	93

Foreword

Many Christians today have a bad conscience about the Bible. They hear it read in church, and described as 'the Word of the Lord'; they find some parts of it inspiring; but they cannot honestly say that it is the book they turn to first when they are perplexed, or the most important source of the hope that is in them. But they know there are people in all the Christian Churches who regard the Bible as an infallible record of divine revelation, and who claim that it directs their every step. Unable to see the Bible in this way themselves, less Bible-centred Christians feel they are missing something. Often they conclude that their faith must be defective. Some of them, burdened with guilt about their inadequate trust in God's Word, drift away from the Christian faith altogether, seeing it as making demands they are not up to. Others simply become exasperated with a religion that seems to demand a sacrifice of common sense and intellectual integrity on the altar of biblical authority. If Christianity depends on believing in an infallible Bible, they feel, so much the worse for Christianity. Either way, the biblicists are left ruling the roost.

But Christians are not really required to choose between fundamentalism and unbelief. Biblicist Christians and opponents of Christianity share a vested interest in making people believe that these are the only alternatives. Fear of atheism can be used to keep believers in the fundamentalist fold, and scorn poured on the obvious absurdities of fundamentalism can discourage agnostics from ever considering the claims of the gospel. But the choice is a false one. This book is written for those who would like to explore another possibility: a positive but critical evaluation of the Bible, which avoids the absolutes of biblicism but is not simply a watered-down version of it.

Thanks are due as always to my wife, Mary, and to Katie, our daughter, for their patience during the preparation of this book and (more importantly) for the happy atmosphere within which it could be written. It is dedicated with love to them both. Many colleagues and friends have helped me to think through, over a long period, the ideas presented here. Some of my thoughts on the Bible began to crystallize in preparing a series of sermons for St

Foreword

Mary Magdalen's, Oxford, as long ago as Advent 1977, and discussions with other members of the Doctrine Commission of the Church of England, to which I belonged from 1978 to 1986, helped me to think them through further. The stimulus provided by the writings of James Barr will be obvious throughout the book – indeed I doubt if I have said anything worth saying that is not anticipated somewhere in his many works on the Bible. Among colleagues in Oxford, Ernest Nicholson has as always been an unfailing source of help, advice and encouragement, and of warm friendship. But no one, of course, is to blame for whatever use I may have made of their ideas.

Much of the reading and preparation for the book was completed during a sabbatical term in Germany, thanks to the generosity of the Theology Faculty Board in Oxford, which made me Denyer and Johnson Travelling Fellow for 1986–7. I am specially indebted to Professor Rudolf Smend, in Göttingen, and to Professors Werner H. Schmidt and Gerhard Sauter in Bonn, the warmth of whose welcome was equal to the academic help they gave me. Much of the first draft was written in Bonn in the house and beautiful garden of Frau G. Herzog, whose generous hospitality is among the happiest memories associated with the writing of this brief assessment of the place of the Bible in the Christian faith.

St Cross College, Oxford
February 1988

PEOPLE OF THE BOOK?

CHAPTER 1

The Bible in the Christian Faith

'Christ is the end of the law'

'People of the Book' is a quotation from the Qur'ān. It is the Qur'ān's name for adherents of what we call the three monotheistic religions, Judaism, Christianity and Islam. In a saying which seems to promise a degree of religious toleration much needed by the modern world in both East and West, the Qur'ān urges the Muslim: 'Do not dispute with the People of the Book: say, we believe in what has been sent down to us and what has been sent down to you; our God and your God is one' (Sura 29.45).

Yet it is really much more problematic to call Christians the 'people of a book' than to call Muslims or even Jews so. There is indeed one group that thinks it knows precisely how Christian faith is related to the Scriptures, a group which at the moment is gaining in strength internationally: the fundamentalists. It is fundamentalism that comes closest to adopting in Christianity a theory of Scripture like the majority Islamic view of the Qur'ān – as supernaturally inspired in origin, inerrant in content, and oracular in function. On the fundamentalist view Christians are indeed a 'people of the book' in the same sense as Muslims, although the book is a different one. Despite the gains by Christian fundamentalism in the last couple of decades, most Christians in Britain are not fundamentalists. But it is increasingly fundamentalism that provides the norms against which theories of the authority of Scripture are tested. In the popular mind biblical authority means the kind of authority that is ascribed to the Bible by fundamentalism, which thus calls the tune to which even its opponents are forced to dance.

For popular fundamentalism knows of only two attitudes to Scripture: its own belief that the Bible is inerrant in everything that it affirms and the sole source of all Christian truth, and what it calls 'liberalism'. What is meant by 'liberalism' is seldom clearly in focus, but usually it is taken to entail a more or less hazy view of Scripture, in which the Bible is believed only on those rare occasions when it happens to coincide with the opinions of 'modern man' – a sceptical and rationalistic person of uncertain religious leanings. Liberal 'modern' men and women in this sense do exist within the religious world. But they are certainly in a tiny minority, and the idea that all non-fundamentalists share their woolliness about the Bible is a conservative myth. Its effect is pernicious, however, for two reasons. First, it forces the non-conservative Christian to spend much time and energy showing why the Bible is not the infallible oracle fundamentalists suppose it to be, and in the process appearing to have a less full-blooded faith than they – to be critical, carping and defensive. And second, it deflects the average person's attention from the fact that most non-conservative, non-fundamentalist Christians do in fact honour and value the Bible. Indeed, they commonly make a much more fruitful and constructive use of it than fundamentalists themselves, who use biblical material with extreme selectivity, under the tight constraints of a doctrinal system that owes little to the biblical text itself, and much to habits of thought every bit as modern and rationalistic as those of so-called liberals.

Thus to show that fundamentalism is wrong can all too easily mean fighting on terrain chosen by the fundamentalist himself, and with much difficulty in persuading the neutral spectator that the high ground is not already occupied by the forces of biblicism. Anti-fundamentalism, though a necessary cause, is in any case a thankless one; for many who are not at all sympathetic to the Christian faith would prefer Christians to be fundamentalists, because that would make it so much easier to reject their religion as absurd.[1] At the same time, however, it is vital not to commit the mistake of thinking that fundamentalists are either stupid or ill-intentioned. Conservative biblicism is an extremely sophisticated movement; its leaders are highly intelligent people with very cool heads. Many who find biblicistic forms of Christianity appealing are also people of strikingly attractive character, with a warm and living faith. That being so, it seems unlikely that the arguments to which they appeal are simply empty. Over the years a suspicion has grown in me that much of the fundamentalists' case is not simply a bad thing, but a good thing gone wrong: they point us towards important truths, but veer away from them themselves at the last moment because a doctrinaire conservatism blinds their eyes. I think I have identified half a dozen places where a raid on conservative arguments might yield treasures for use in a non-conservative, critical theory of biblical authority. And for the many Christians who (like me) have no time for biblicism, and yet love the Bible, there is a pressing need for such a theory.

Pride of place must go to the conservative belief that the earliest Christians, and indeed Jesus himself, must be the arbiters of any Christian doctrine of Scripture. This will concern us in the remainder of this chapter. A more specific form of it, which appeals to the idea of prophecy and fulfilment, will be discussed in chapter 2. These two chapters will thus concentrate primarily on the authority of the Old Testament. In chapters 3 and 4 we consider the question of the canon (a basket into which many conservative eggs are being packed at the moment), and the Bible as a source of evidence. The remaining chapters examine the Bible as a book of faith (chapter 5), hermeneutical theories of the meaning of Scripture (chapter 6), and its function in Christian worship (chapter 7). In every case we hope to show that aspects of Scripture to which fundamentalists insistently point can be better allies in the cause of a constructive non-conservative theory of Scripture than they are in what seems to so many their natural conservative habitat. In this way it may be possible to find a basis for construction which is not dictated by polemical concerns and yet avoids the risk of appearing to make no contact with what, after all, seems to many the most full-blooded form of Christian belief in scriptural authority.

Of course we know in advance that any such discussion will be called liberal by fundamentalists themselves. I hardly expect to be thanked if I succeed in stealing their best tunes. But I am convinced that a robust theory of Scripture is possible without selling out to biblicism. The Bible, after all, is and always has been an essential resource to which Christians ceaselessly return in the certainty of being refreshed and nourished. As the translators of the Authorized Version put it:

The Scripture is a tree, or rather a whole paradise of trees of life, which bring forth fruits every month, and the fruit thereof is for meat, and the leaves for medicine. It is not a pot of manna or a cruse of oil, which were for memory only, or for a meal's meat or two, but as it were a shower of heavenly bread sufficient for a whole host, be it never so great, and as it were a whole cellarful of oil vessels; whereby all our necessities may be provided for, and our debts discharged. In a word it is a pantry of wholesome food against mouldy traditions; a pharmacist's shop (Saint Basil calleth it) of preservatives against poisoned heresies; a code of profitable laws against rebellious spirits; a treasury of most costly jewels against beggarly rudiments. Finally, a fountain of most pure water springing up into everlasting life.[2]

The question for a Christian is not *whether* this is so, but *how* it is so. What is the relation between our knowledge of God and the Bible which thus mysteriously seems to nourish this knowledge in us? How should Christians think of the Bible?

I

The first of the conservative contributions to this question we must consider consists of a simple and direct appeal to the earliest

Christian traditions. We should think about the Bible, it is argued, exactly what the first Christians thought about it. Theologians are usually wary of committing themselves to a proposition as bald as this; but for my part I cannot see how it can be faulted. Rather than water it down, let us grant it, but ask where it leads. What was in fact believed about Scripture in the early years of the Christian faith?

Already in the second and third generations Christianity knew of tensions and disagreements about the Bible. At one extreme a quasi-fundamentalist idea of Old Testament Scripture as an ultimate and unerring authority does have clear echoes in the thinking of Christians of the first few generations. St Matthew's Gospel, in the second half of the first century, presents a Jesus who insisted on the binding force of 'the Law and the Prophets', that is, of the existing Scriptures – the Old Testament, give or take a book or two (see Matt. 5.17–20). By the next generation we find Christian writers who have already so completely baptized the Old Testament as the Church's Scriptures that they can appeal to it as an absolutely persuasive argument for the minutiae of church order. We can see this, for example, in the so-called Epistle of Barnabas, or in the First Epistle of Clement (the third successor of Peter at Rome) which cites lengthy chunks of the Bible to support its appeals for the government of the Church by bishops and deacons – much like a Puritan of the seventeenth century using Old Testament laws about the government of Israel to insist on a presbyterian polity for the Christian congregation (see Barnabas 6.11–12, 13; 1 Clement 42).

But at the other extreme there were those who were prepared to reject altogether the use of the Old Testament as a court of appeal. It was argued that an appeal to the Old Testament failed to do justice to the newness of the revelation in Christ; alternatively, or additionally, that it ignored the existence in the Church of continually renewed revelation through the activity of the Holy Spirit, providing prophetic utterances and guiding Christians into new truth. Both these objections to the old Scriptures may be seen in a passage of St Ignatius of Antioch from the very beginning of the second century. Ignatius has encountered a group of Christians who say that they will not believe anything 'in the [preaching of the] gospel' unless they can find it in 'our ancient records', that is, in the Scriptures of the Old Testament. Ignatius, in what sounds like a radical rejection of the old Scriptures, replies that for him the 'records' are not written texts at all, but 'Jesus Christ; for me, the sacrosanct records are the cross and death and resurrection of Jesus Christ, and the faith that comes through him'.[3] These are the norms by which Christians live, and according to which Scripture itself is to be judged. And Ignatius is true to his principles in referring very little to the Old Testament. The attitude he condemns is probably what the early Church called 'judaizing': that is, a failure to think through the consequences of St Paul's claim that Christians were free from the constraints of the Jewish religious system, and a feeling that to become a Christian one must first become a Jew and so accept the full weight of Jewish Scripture. Against this attiitude Ignatius felt that the newness of Christ, and the indwelling of the Holy Spirit in the Church, made any documents superfluous and any authority that lay in the past deeply suspect.

Now admittedly this type of opposition to the old Scriptures was not much like the modern 'liberalism' of fundamentalist fantasy. Its 'anti-judaizing' strand ends in Marcionism, a second-century 'gnostic' heresy, where opposition to the Old Testament and Judaism was part of a rejection of the creator-god and all his works as evil, and Christ was revered as having established a religion of salvation from the taints of the flesh.[4] This is a style of Christianity, if indeed it is Christianity at all, which scarcely exists today. The second strand, emphasis on a Spirit-filled Church which needs no Scriptures, is more like the left wing of the Reformation than it is like modern 'liberal' Christianity: it is the religion of wild extremists, not of comfortable liberals. The second-century debate about the Bible was thus not the same as our modern debates. But already the Bible was clearly a battleground for opposing factions, not a serenely accepted authority. Thus an appeal to the example of the earliest Christians as a basis for insisting on an unquestioning acceptance of Scripture begins to look shaky.

II

But all this, it may be said, is nothing to the point. If we go back *behind* these debates of the second and third generations, and return to the clear teaching of St Paul and, indeed, of Jesus himself, all will be plain. This, alas, is the vainest of hopes. In the epistles of St Paul in the 40s and 50s of the first century, and in the sayings of Jesus in the synoptic Gospels, we are presented not merely with a degree of tension but with what is, in terms of later debates, an irreconcilable contradiction. To put it briefly, in both cases we seem to find what look like signs of *both* traditions of thought, the pro-Scripture and the anti-Scripture, not as the opinions of warring factions, but as elements within the thinking of one and the same person. Only if we grasp this nettle can we hope to take our earliest of all sources seriously; yet, as I shall argue, if we do grasp it, we can find a way out of the sterility to which the modern debate between fundamentalists and so-called liberals has condemned us.

To take Paul first: on the one hand, his interest in the Old Testament seems at best intermittent and casual. As Hans von Campenhausen (following Adolf von Harnack[5]) stresses in his important study *The Formation of the Christian Bible*, several of Paul's shorter epistles contain scarcely a reference to Scripture.[6] The argument proceeds entirely without any felt need to relate Christian experience to scriptural revelation, and Paul seems to regard what has come about in Jesus as so new, and so all-embracing, that there is no thought of justifying or qualifying it by reference to any already existing Scripture. In commending the faith to Gentile Christians, Paul felt no need to begin with Jewish Scripture, or even to bring Scripture in at a later stage. The Christian message was self-contained and had its own logic. It was in no sense an interpretation of what was already written, but a fresh input by God to be grasped and interpreted on its own terms. When Marcion came later to establish his 'pure' Pauline canon, purged of all Old Testament allusions, there were some epistles he hardly needed to revise, for they were already in his terms ideologically pure.

This seems at first glance just what we should expect from Paul's rejection of the 'Law'. We can understand how Schleiermacher was able to say 'we might call [Paul] as a witness in support of the position that Old Testament proofs are no longer required'.[7] And yet the surprising truth is that Paul's Gentile mission, and attendant rejection of 'the works of the Law', did not at all make him opposed to the existing Scriptures, in the manner of Marcion or even of Ignatius. On the contrary, when Paul does quote from the Old Testament, he clearly regards its divine origin and consequent authority not only as certain but as quite unproblematic and self-evident. The so-called 'argument from prophecy', which will concern us in the next chapter, occurs very little in Paul; but when it does appear there is not the slightest hint of discomfort. Scripture says it, therefore it must be so. Nothing Paul says about the abrogation of the Law seems to affect in the least his veneration for the words of the Old Testament, which are the oracles of God himself. As Otto Michel put it some sixty years ago in his study of St Paul and his Bible, 'There is not a single warning in the Pauline literature that the Old Testament should be used carefully, or should take second place to some other means of edification.'[8] Paul's 'gospel' included from the first 'that Christ died for our sins *in accordance with the scriptures*, [and] . . . that he was raised on the third day *in accordance with the scriptures*' (1 Cor. 15.3–4): the Scriptures (that is, the Old Testament) are there from the beginning.

Now we should agree with von Campenhausen that 'the only route [Paul] knows runs from Christ to knowledge of the Scriptures, and its direction cannot be reversed'.[9] Certainly it is false to say, as Paul Ricoeur (for example) has done, that the early Christian message is *primarily* or predominantly a hermeneutic of the Old Testament.[10] For the first Christians, what had happened in Christ was not an exegesis of Scripture, not even a strikingly original exegesis of Scripture, but a completely new, unprecedented and irreversible event in the external world. It was not primarily something that had happened inside a tradition of textual interpretation. The interpretation of existing Scripture had to limp along as best it could to catch up, and it had no power to annul the new thing that God had accomplished. But on the other hand, this emphatically did not result in a sense that Scripture had been replaced or overturned – not even for Paul, who in his criticism of existing Scripture as an adequate basis for a relationship with God goes as far as any early Christian writer, and much farther than most. 'Christ is the end of the law' (Rom. 10.4); yet the Law, including all the old Scriptures which went with it, remained the oracles of God, entrusted to the Jewish people; and 'the gifts and the call of God are irrevocable' (Rom. 11.29).

Much of the argument of Romans, of course, is notoriously complex, and we might simply want to say that Paul was muddled. He embraced the principle that ought to have led him simply to reject the Old Testament out of hand as superseded, but he was too confused, perhaps even too cautious, to follow the logic of his own argument. Consequently he failed to liberate Christians as fully from the domination of the Old Testament as he should have done. Harnack saw this as the great failure of nerve on the part of the apostolic Church, with baneful effects down to the present day.[11] Yet Paul does not appear to be embarrassed by his acceptance of the authority of the Old Testament. In this he seems in accord with Jesus himself. However we may reconstruct Jesus' teaching, two things are surely plain enough. On the one hand, he did not regularly or even commonly teach by scriptural exposition, but through proverbs, parables and free reflections on experience and social life – Paul, indeed, seems to have done the same. Nor was Jesus' teaching about God's imminent intervention – the coming 'Kingdom of God' – based on scriptural exegesis, but on a claim to have received direct divine revelation; and again, exactly the same may be said of Paul. Yet on the other hand, the authority and divine inspiration of the Scriptures was not at all in question. What we call the Old Testament was for Jesus unquestionably the word of his Father. Where we do hear Jesus engaged in disputes about Scripture, it is where he champions it against subsequent human tradition (as, for example, in Mark 7.9–13); or where, as in the sayings on divorce, he appeals to it as giving insight into God's original purposes for his world (Mark 10.2–9 and parallels). In Jesus' thought, apparently, God is speaking a new word through him, both in his teaching and in his actions, yet the authority and inspiration of God's former words is not felt as an embarrassment.

Thus, if we turn to the earliest of all witnesses to the gospel, we are immediately faced with a puzzle. Within the lines of debate as currently drawn up, it looks as if we shall have to say that the liberals and the fundamentalists are both right: everybody has won, and all must have prizes. Yet fundamentalist and so-called 'liberal' positions as we know them certainly cannot be reconciled, and the attempt to hold them together causes tensions and discomforts of which there is not the smallest hint in either Paul or his Master. The answer must surely be that the authority of Scripture meant something radically different for them from what it means for most modern people. And it may be worth trying to recapture a model for understanding the function of Scripture within which the attitudes evinced in the teaching of Jesus and Paul are thinkable and even natural. There is, of course, no guarantee that this model will prove viable in our own day. But it seems worthwhile to discover what it might be, if we are to continue to worship the God who is known through Christ and yet who 'in many and various ways . . . spoke of old to our fathers by the prophets' (Heb. 1.1). To turn again to von Campenhausen: 'Christianity is no longer a "religion of a book", in the strict sense of that phrase, since Christians believe in the lordship of the living Christ and in the present reality of the Spirit.'[12] Yet Christians remained in some sense 'people of the book', and it seems that they would have failed in loyalty to the lordship of Christ if they had simply cast off the old Scriptures in their joyful acceptance of the new revelation. What is the key that will unlock this mystery?

III

The bare outline of an answer, which we shall develop in subsequent chapters, might run as follows. The relation of the faith which Christians profess to the Scripture which informs and nourishes that faith is not just accidentally or occasionally but essentially and inherently one of tension. St Paul's attitude, indeed the attitude of Jesus himself in so far as we can discover it, is not an incoherent or halfway-house attitude; it is bound up with an essential feature of the gospel proclamation. The Christian gospel is a message about both creation and redemption; about two stages in God's dealings with his world; about the way in which (as the ancient collect puts it) God wonderfully created the dignity of human nature but then yet more wonderfully restored it. The ambiguous relation of the new to the old is not an accidental aspect of the gospel message, but an essential part of it.

The Christian gospel is not that a new God, never before known, has just been revealed in Jesus. It is that the God who already is known has, nevertheless, just done something new and unprecedented – something which means nothing less than the remaking of the world. In relation to the Old Testament, this implies that there can be no Christianity without it and yet none that knows it alone. In relation to the New Testament (when a New Testament eventually formed), it meant that there could be no fresh impulses from the Holy Spirit that contradicted the revelation in Christ recorded there; and yet – precisely because the Spirit is active and makes all things new – there could never be a mere conservatism of the written letter. Luther no doubt exaggerated the opposition of law and gospel, but his contrast did correctly grasp something that is at the heart of the gospel: that there are two dispensations in the providence of God, and that the second, the one that begins with Christ and continues through the work of the Holy Spirit in the Church and in the world, is predicated on a contrast with the first. This contrast is not (as Lutherans sometimes seem to suggest) purely by way of opposition and abolition, it is also by way of completion and addition: Christ is the end of 'the Law' not simply as its replacement but also in some sense as its culmination. Contrast there must be; but there can be a contrast only if the old remains in existence even after the new has come. Otherwise we have simply a new religion, or a religion that is forever changing into something different.

The gospel says that in Christ God has as it were annulled his own laws, set aside his own demands, indeed created the world anew: 'if any one is in Christ, he is a new creation; the old has passed away; behold, the new has come' (2 Cor. 5.17). But if we therefore simply *forget* the old, the new loses its newness. Contrast is of the essence of the gospel, and in this the retention of the old Scriptures is an essential step. They are retained because the God who was known through them is the true God and it is he – not some other god – who has just acted in ways these same Scriptures had not foreseen.

The tension between the new faith and the old Scriptures therefore is not a *problem*, but part of the essence of Christianity from the beginning. Christians are people who have a book, in order to be able to proclaim their freedom from it; yet the character of that freedom is deeply shaped by the book from which they have been freed, and it is the God who gave the book who also gives the freedom. Rudolf Smend puts it like this:

> In Jesus the fullness of the covenant which in the Old Testament was broken by the disobedience of Israel and which had survived, despite all human efforts, only in the form of promise, became a reality; in him God and man are at one. He is the goal, but also the end, the end, yet also the goal, of Yahweh's way with Israel and Israel's with Yahweh. In this statement of faith there lies our yes to the Old Testament, but also our no; our no, yet also our yes, as a way of repeating God's own gracious yes after him – and hence also his gracious no.[13]

These are hard sayings; we will try to explain them in the chapters that follow. Meanwhile, here is an early reflection on the paradox, Melito of Sardis' Paschal Homily, from about a century after St Paul:

> Understand, therefore, beloved, that the Paschal mystery is both new and old; eternal and temporary; perishable and imperishable; mortal and immortal. It is old as regards the law, but new as regards the Spirit; temporary in respect of the model, but eternal because of grace; mortal because of the Lord's burial in earth, yet immortal because of his rising from the dead.[14]

Notes

1. The definitive case against fundamentalism in our day has been assembled by James Barr in his two books *Fundamentalism*, London 1977, second edn 1981, and *Escaping from Fundamentalism*, London 1984. See also his *The Bible in the Modern World* (London 1973), pp. 168–71 and 'The Problem of Fundamentalism Today' in his *Explorations in Theology 7: The Scope and Authority of the Bible* (London 1980), pp. 65–90.

2. From the 'Address to the Reader' prefixed to the Authorized (King James) Version of the Bible of 1611. Cf. J. Muddiman, *The Bible: Fountain and Well of Truth* (Oxford 1983), p. 7: 'Scripture is a fountain of truth. Mysteriously in the presence of the risen Christ, the truth behind the text can rise to the surface of its own accord, and be apprehended in all its freshness and immediacy. The Bible has this mysterious or 'sacramental' quality; it can become the vehicle of communication with the Spirit of God.' John Muddiman's short book is one of the best modern statements of a constructive critical approach to the Bible.

3. Ignatius, *Philadelphians* 8; tr. M. Staniforth, rev. A. Louth in *Early Christian Writings: The Apostolic Fathers* (London 1987), p. 95.

4. On Marcion and the formation of the biblical canon see H. von Campenhausen, 'Marcion et les origines du canon néotestamentaire', *Revue d'histoire et de philosophie religieuses* 46 (1966), pp. 213–26 and *The Formation of the Christian Bible* (London 1972), pp. 147–82. Marcion's New Testament contained only an (expurgated) Gospel of Luke and certain Pauline epistles, with all Old Testament quotations removed.

5. See A. von Harnack, *Das Alte Testament in den paulinischen Briefen und in den paulinischen Gemeinden*, Berlin 1928.

6. von Campenhausen, *Formation*, p. 25.

7. F. D. E. Schleiermacher, *The Christian Faith* (Edinburgh 1956), p. 610.

8. O. Michel, *Paulus und seine Bibel* (Gütersloh 1929), p. 118 (my translation).

9. von Campenhausen, *Formation*, p. 29.

10. See P. Ricoeur, *Essays on Biblical Interpretation*, ed. L. S. Mudge (Philadelphia 1980, London 1981), p. 51. Cf. the comment of James Barr in *Holy Scripture: Canon, Authority, Criticism* (Philadelphia and Oxford, 1983), p. 70: 'It was a pleasant joke to say that the New Testament was the first good commentary on the Bible, but it was never anything more than a joke. Taken seriously, it was damaging, for it suggested that the relation between the Old and the New Testaments was basically a hermeneutic one. Ricoeur exaggerates when he says that "the kerygma is the rereading of an ancient scripture": one could rightly say that the kerygma permits or enables or encourages the rereading of an ancient scripture, but it is not in essence such a rereading.'

11. cf. Harnack's celebrated remark (from his *Marcion. Das Evangelium vom fremden Gott. Eine Monographie zur Geschichte der katholischen Kirche* (Berlin 1921, pp. 248–9; my translation): 'To reject the Old Testament in the second century was a mistake which the Church rightly repudiated; to retain it in the sixteenth century was a fate which the Reformation could not yet avoid; but to continue to keep it as a canonical document after the nineteenth century is the consequence of religious and ecclesiastical paralysis.'

12. von Campenhausen, *Formation*, p. 1.

13. R. Smend, 'Die Mitte des Alten Testaments', *Theologische Studien* Beiheft 101; reprinted in R. Smend, *Die Mitte des Alten Testaments*, Beiträge zur evangelischen Theologie 99 (Munich 1986), pp. 40–84; the quotation is from p. 83 (my translation).

14. See S. G. Hall, ed., *Melito* On Pasch *and Fragments* (Oxford 1979), p. 2; my translation.

CHAPTER 2

Prophecy and Fulfilment

*****

'According to the Scriptures'

Debates among Christians about the authority of the Bible frequently work with a contrast between the ages of faith in which, it is supposed, scriptural authority was unproblematic, and the post-Enlightenment world of scepticism and rationalism. From the conservative side, this contrast is deployed in order to call the Church back to the Bible. But for those with more critical leanings the same contrast is a means of explaining why simple biblicism is simply inadequate in the vastly changed conditions of the modern world. For this second group, the question of scriptural authority then becomes the question of what *residual* authority Scripture can be held to possess, how far we can still *even so* believe in the Bible at least to some respectable extent. So long as the question is understood like this, however, the conservatives are bound to win the propaganda war, and they have many glorious opportunities for fighting with their favourite weapon, the thin end of the wedge. Critical theology plays into their hands if it approaches the matter in this way, for it tacitly acknowledges that a really robust theory of scriptural authority would have to be the fundamentalist one, and it has to keep giving its own much more anaemic version transfusions of blood from more and more dubious sources to keep the contest going.

In the last chapter I tried to put the debate out of the reach of the fundamentalists' wedge by proposing that we take their concern for the ages of faith with sufficient seriousness to return absolutely *ad fontes*, and consult the teachings of St Paul and of Jesus himself. I suggested that the effect of this would be to redefine the questions it made sense to ask about scriptural authority. Instead of finding there the high and absolute biblicism favoured by conservatives, we find an overwhelming sense that God has just done (or is just doing or is just about to do) something so new that Scripture cannot contain it, and could never have led anyone to foresee it. At the same time, however, we do *not* find this leading to the conclusion that Scripture (that is, in this context, the Old Testament) is now dispensable. Serious recourse to Jesus and Paul thus makes a fundamentalist position hard to maintain, but

12

not by simply proving that an anti-scriptural liberalism is right instead. Rather, attention to the earliest witnesses suggests that the conservative–'liberal' debate is missing the point, and that the idea of the authority of Scripture has somehow been garbled by both sides in our present debates. The authority of the Old Testament, in particular, is an inherently ambiguous one in Christianity, and attempts to remove the ambiguity produce a distortion of the gospel.

We can see this in more detail if we survey one early Christian theory which tried to resolve the tension between new and old by arguing that (in the words of Augustine's well-known tag) 'the new is concealed in the old, the old revealed in the new', and that both are harmonious parts of a single authoritative Christian Bible. This theory is the argument from the fulfilment of ancient prophecy in Christ – an argument which looks at first sight as if it presupposes the absolute authority of the old Scriptures for Christians. For that very reason it remains dear to the hearts of biblical conservatives.

I

Ostensibly the argument from prophecy works by saying that there is an enormous agreed stock of messianic predictions in the Old Testament, and then showing that Jesus rather than anyone else is the person in whom they have 'come true'. His life, death and resurrection correspond with these predictions point by point. However, the working out of the argument in practice throws up all kinds of problems. Not only are there the well-known difficulties about attributing to God detailed predictions of the future; there are also far subtler questions about the underlying attitude to Scripture, which is in reality far more complex than simple biblicists suppose. For very few Christians, however biblically conservative, now seriously try to use the argument from prophecy in dialogue with Jews; and the reason why it fails is not that Jews cannot be argued into agreeing that it is indeed Jesus who fulfils the prophecies on the agreed common syllabus. It is that they do not agree on the syllabus.

Of all the Old Testament 'prophecies', none is dearer to Christian hearts than that of Isaiah 52.13—53.12, a passage read in many Christian churches on Good Friday, which speaks of the sufferings of the Servant of the Lord:

> He was despised and rejected by men;
>   a man of sorrows, and acquainted with grief . . .
>
> Surely he has borne our griefs
>   and carried our sorrows . . .

13

He was wounded for our transgressions,
    he was bruised for our iniquities;
upon him was the chastisement that made us whole,
    and with his stripes we are healed.

Modern critical scholarship has often been blamed by conservative Christians for having decreed that this is not in origin a
'messianic prophecy' at all, but a mysterious description of some
figure contemporary with the author (an anonymous prophet of
the sixth century BC now conventionally called 'Deutero-Isaiah').
But from time immemorial Jews have rejected the messianic
interpretation. It has sometimes been seen as a prediction of the
Messiah in some strands of Jewish thought, but has very seldom
been a focal point for Jewish hopes. In mainstream Judaism the
passage is not the subject of assiduous exegetical work designed
to show that it does not refer to Christ, because it is not regarded
as a messianic prophecy anyway. The same may be said of Jeremiah's prophecy of a new covenant (Jer. 31), of most of the
'messianic' prophecies in the Psalms, and of the verses which
Christians have read as prophecies of the resurrection of the
dead, such as Ezekiel's vision of the valley of dry bones (Ezek.
37.1–14). All are in any case quite marginal in Jewish reading
of Scripture, where it is generally the Torah (the Pentateuch),
not the prophetic books or the Psalms, that holds the centre of
attention.

The argument from prophecy miscarries, not so much because
people cannot be convinced that only Jesus fulfils the prophecies,
as because they cannot be convinced that the texts he is supposed
to fulfil are messianic prophecies anyway. From the New Testament writers onwards, we find Christians who want to deploy
the argument from prophecy forced to engage in lengthy pre-
liminary arguments, often of great exegetical subtlety, in order
first to demonstrate that the texts which Christ is said to fulfil are
indeed predictions that need fulfilment. We can see the process
in some of the speeches in the early chapters of Acts. For example, Peter cites Psalm 16 ('Thou wilt not abandon my soul to
Hades, nor let thy Holy One see corruption'), and argues that it
cannot refer to David, the psalmist, because David died and was
buried and *did* see corruption: therefore it must refer to some
future person who would not be corrupted in the grave; and
Christ's resurrection shows that he is that person (Acts 2.25–36;
cf. also 13.35–7). Or take Hebrews 3–4, commenting on the words
of Psalm 95.11: 'I swore in my wrath, "They shall never enter my
rest."' The 'rest' referred to here is first shown, with great
ingenuity, not to have been granted in the event which Jewish
tradition saw as a giving of rest to a homeless people – that is, the

conquest of Palestine under Joshua. This is said in order to establish that the psalm-text is therefore really a prophecy of some future event, and thus to present it as a text still awaiting its fulfilment. *Only then* can the author go on to argue that the true 'rest' which really will fulfil the Psalm is the 'rest' which Jesus gives to his followers.

In cases like these, it is not so much that the Christian dispensation is being shown to fulfil old prophecy, as that Christian faith is *generating* prophecies out of the words of an old text which originally had no reference to the future at all. Christian apologetic is not a matter of showing that Jesus fulfils prophecy, but of finding prophecies for Jesus to fulfil.[1]

The early Christian argument from prophecy was seldom in reality part of a dialogue with Jews. Usually it belonged to teaching within the Church, and was designed to support the faith which Christians already had, rather than being real apologetic. The imaginary opponents who are being talked into accepting the idea that certain texts are prophecies of Christ are not real Jewish commentators, but straw men, mere foils for the purpose of the argument. In this the 'prophecies' and their fulfilment supported each other: that what God foretells comes true, and that what comes true is what he has foretold, these were arguments of equal weight in the Christian mind.

By the time we reach the Epistle of Barnabas in (probably) the second century, the fulfilment pattern means that the continuity between the old revelation and the new is perfect and seamless, and there is in no sense a *problem* of the Old Testament. Thus, for example, Barnabas takes it as a matter of course that everything said to Israel, or indeed to mankind, in the Old Testament is really aimed at the Christian community. Perhaps this is most startling in the following passage:

> When [God] turned us into new men by the remission of our sins, it made us into men of a wholly different stamp – having so completely the souls of little children that it seemed as though he had created us all over again. It is with reference to *our* refashioning that Scripture makes him say to his Son, 'Let us make man in our own image and likeness; and let them rule over the beasts of the earth, and the fowls of the air, and the fishes of the sea'; adding, as he contemplated the beauty of *our* fashioning, 'Increase, and multiply, and fill the earth'.[2]

The new creation here simply swallows up the first, even the command to 'increase and multiply' being allegorized as a command to spread the gospel. The author has absolutely no sense

15

that the Old Testament is the record of pre-Christian Israel; it is simply through and through a Christian book.

The form which the argument from prophecy normally takes in early Christianity is thus not such as to imply that the Old Testament Scriptures were really the true source of authority: this is the point we are driving at. It was *Christ*, as understood by the Church, who determined not only how the prophecies were fulfilled but even which texts were regarded as prophetic in the first place. This is the clearest case of the imposition of a Christological perspective on the Old Testament. As the so-called Clementine Recognitions all too candidly put it, 'Jesus is not to be believed because the prophets foretold him, but rather the prophets are to be believed to be true prophets, because Christ bore witness to them.'[3] The old Scriptures remain in force only because they no longer speak with their own voice: they are turned into a collection of texts whose words express what is in reality a wholly new message. The very status which is accorded to the Old Testament precludes it from being heard, because it is turned into a collection of Christian texts whose real meaning is as it were encoded under forms that appear – but only to the uninitiated – to be the forms of the old Jewish religion.

But the price for such a solution was a very high one. The early Church was not troubled by the element in this way of thinking which is perhaps most deeply unsettling for the modern Christian: its entire failure to make any theological sense of Judaism as a continuing religion. 'The Jews' for Barnabas, as indeed for the author of Hebrews and some other New Testament writers, are not clearly in focus as a contemporary group. By 'the Jews' he means the ancient Israelites, who are more or less taken to have come to an end now that the new Israel is here. He speaks of the rejection of the generation that made the golden calf as though this self-evidently meant that God had no time for the Jews of Jesus' day, or of his own either. Ancient Israel, first-century Judaism and the continuing Jewish religion are simply one thing, a thing hated by God. A Christian in the second half of the twentieth century will of course be extremely uncomfortable with so negative a judgement on Judaism, but will also wonder whether an acceptance of the Old Testament on such terms is not really a destruction of it.

The status which the argument from prophecy ascribes to the Old Testament thus seems very dearly bought, for these books remained 'canonical' only at the cost of their independence and facticity as ancient Jewish Scripture. They were not, we may say, allowed to *remain* canonical; they were forcibly baptized. The argument from prophecy showed that the Old Testament properly understood was simply a Christian book. The Jews, so it was argued, did not understand it because, in Paul's words, 'a veil lies over their minds', and they refused to be convinced that Christ is its fulfilment. Paul himself more than once explicitly states the principle involved here: 'whatever was written in former days was written for *our* instruction' (Rom. 15.4); 'these things . . . were written down for *our* instruction, upon whom the end of the ages has come' (1 Cor. 10.11; cf. 9.10).

When once people started to read the Old Testament on its own terms (as they did, however falteringly, at the Reformation), then it became clear that by such arguments the Church had painted itself into a corner. For the Old Testament is of course not a Christian book in this direct sense at all. It is a Jewish book, sometimes compatible with the New Testament, sometimes incompatible, more often than not simply engaging with different questions. If the ground for accepting it in the Church was to be the argument from prophecy, the argument that it pointed to Christ, then there were only two escape routes from this corner; and both led into outer darkness. One was to assert against all appearances that everything in the Jewish Scriptures did indeed point to Christ, that is, that Christianity should be adapted to accommodate it all. This is the door through which most modern fundamentalists have passed. It leads to what Lutherans would call the 'judaizing' of the gospel, the assumption that from even the most unpromising portions of Old Testament law exegetical labour can wrest commands for Christians to obey and doctrines for them to believe, and woe betide them if they do not. The other door is marked with the name of Luther himself, and leads to a world where whatever in the Old Testament does not seem to point to Christ is simply rejected. Whatever was spoken in Judaism, if it was not repeated by Christ, should not be deemed to have been spoken by God; it was a mere shadow, a human deceit, the voice of unredeemed humanity. And through that door the freedom of the gospel seems to beckon, but it is a gospel stained with much Jewish blood spilt by an anti-semitism claiming the name of Jesus as its justification.

Once we allow the argument from prophecy to be the measure of our acceptance of the Old Testament, and yet feel constrained to attend to the natural sense of the text, we shall find ourselves hard put to it to avoid one or other of these unappealing choices: to deny that Christ transforms the religion into which he came, or else to deny that that religion was truly in touch with the living God. And nothing worth calling Christian can survive either course.

II

Thus the argument from prophecy seems to have run us into a cul-de-sac. But though the argument is certainly found all over the New Testament, and (as we have seen) Paul knew it, and accepted its theoretical basis, yet there are other strains of thought in the New Testament besides; and in Paul perhaps above all. Von Campenhausen writes:

> Certainly, Paul too maintains that the sending of Christ is in accordance with the divine plan of salvation, and thus with the 'Scriptures' . . . But the later, typical form of the proof from Scripture, which confirms the claims of Christ by demonstrating the oracular agreement of particular details from the life of Jesus with the corresponding prophecies of the Old Testament, does not occur in Paul.[4]

We expect to find it, especially if we are thinking of the picture of Paul in Acts, where he is often presented as arguing from prophecy in the same manner as other Christian apologists. But in the epistles it virtually never occurs. The messianic status of Jesus, his eschatological significance, his death and resurrection and the salvation they have accomplished, these are not argued from scriptural proofs. And yet Paul remains convinced that the old Scriptures are the Word of God. For his reading of the Old Testament is really much less Christocentric than any reading which takes its point of departure from the argument from prophecy.

Paul seems to represent a stage before the complex baptism of the whole Old Testament in detail had begun, a more relaxed and uncomplicated stage in Christian thought about Scripture. Very few of the texts he does cite and discuss are chosen because of a 'prophecy and fulfilment' scheme. Often he will bring in an Old Testament text merely to support an argument reached by other routes – this is specially common in his sections of ethical teaching. In this there is not much to choose between the way he cites Scripture and the way he cites popular proverbs or commonplaces. As we noted in the last chapter, Paul, like Jesus, often appeals to everyday experience and draws out moral or religious consequences – say, from the conventions of military service or ordinary employment, as in 1 Corinthians 9.7.[5] One often has the impression that his use of Scripture is equally informal, and indicates merely that it was part of the air he breathed, rather than being cited as an 'authority'.

Biblical texts often provide convenient tags, hallowed ways of expressing pithily something Paul wants to say on other grounds. Thus for example in 1 Corinthians 1.18–19 his argument about the foolishness of God and the wisdom of men is summed up in a saying from Isaiah 29.14, 'I will destroy the wisdom of the wise, and the cleverness of the clever I will thwart.' This is hardly a predictive prophecy coming true: that is an exaggerated way of taking it. It is simply a scriptural way of expressing God's characteristic mode of action, of which the cross of Christ is held up as the supreme example. Scripture is here providing Paul with his vocabulary, not with prophecies looking for fulfilment. Even in the second century, von Campenhausen argues, not all Christian writers adopted the 'hard' form of the argument from prophecy which would cause the difficulties for modern Christians we have been describing. Even as late as 1 Clement 'such "scriptural proofs" were handled with freedom because they were thought of more as edificatory than as legalistic or dogmatic'.[6] Much the same may be said of Paul. Of course he can also torture the biblical text to make it support his own argument;[7] but his relation to Scripture is for the most part much looser and more informal than this, and leaves vast tracts of the old texts uninterpreted and so unchristianized. We cannot, as we can with later exegetes such as Origen, work out from first principles how Paul would have interpreted passages he does not actually use: he has no consistent and generalized hermeneutic of the Old Testament. In itself this may not seem particularly important. But in a modern religious context, where much stress is being placed by conservative Christians on the Bible as an utterly authoritative and binding, verbally-inspired reference book, the informality, indeed casualness, of Paul's use of it is deeply significant.

III

Once the Old Testament Scriptures had been (so to speak) 'naturalized' in the Church, they acquired the status and began to present the problems which Christians have found in them ever since, because they came to constitute a holy book with no context of its own, only the new and artificial context provided between the covers of a single 'Christian Bible'. They were ostensibly the absolutely authoritative divine revelation; but in reality they functioned as a *tabula rasa* on which Christians wrote what they took (on quite other grounds) to be the meaning of Christ. Theoretical authority went hand in hand with actual inefficacy, since they read the Old Testament very much as if its authors had all been Christians who merely expressed themselves rather obliquely. The result was what Maurice Wiles has called an overexegesis.[8] The Bible had acquired, like the holy books of many religions, a certain *semantic indeterminacy*, as a function of its very status. Since it enshrined the truth, it had to be read as saying what one already believed the truth to be. Thus it became, in the phrase Benjamin Jowett borrowed from the Waldensians, '"*Gallus in campanili*, the weathercock on the church tower", which is turned hither and thither by every wind of doctrine'.[9] This semantic indeterminacy of sacred texts will be a continuing theme in this book.

But for Paul, and indeed for Jesus himself, to see the Old Testament in this way was as yet an impossibility. For both of them, the old Scriptures were not yet a self-contained book which Christians could annexe and read as they chose. They were the sacred writings of a religious, cultural, ethical, political and intellectual system within which the Christian movement had begun and towards which it had to take some attitude. What matters, we may say, for Paul as for Jesus himself is not 'what Scripture says' in a kind of vacuum, but how God's fresh input into the human situation in Jesus is to be related to the relationship he already had with the human race, focused through Israel. Of this relationship the Scriptures we call the Old Testament are of course the primary literary deposit. But they do not exhaust it or amount to a total registration of it.

To put it another way: the question whether Jesus fulfils Old Testament prophecy is in reality an artificial question; and the fact that it has never been a fruitful question to ask in genuine Jewish–Christian dialogue is a function of this artificiality. The question which mattered for Paul was not whether Jesus did or did not fulfil – that is, correspond point by point to – discrete predictions that could be lifted out of the Old Testament, but rather how Jesus related to the structures, the hopes and the experience of God in Judaism. To say that this is a question about the relation of Christian faith to 'the Old Testament' or 'to Scripture' is for everyday purposes a harmless enough way of putting it. Of course many varieties of Judaism in the first century were already to a considerable extent the religion of a book, treating the Bible, especially the Pentateuch, with enormous reverence. But for all that, it can be a misleading way of putting it, if we take this too literally and straightforwardly as a question about the relation of Christianity to a sacred text. Really primitive Christianity was deeply concerned, not with the exegesis of bits of a holy text, but with the knowledge of God which had been communicated, it was believed, through the teaching, death and resurrection of Jesus, and with how this was to be made sense of against the background of that knowledge of God which the Jews had already received. This knowledge was by no means identical with the text of the Old Testament. It included much that is not now in

Scripture at all, and de-emphasized much that is.[10] This is a larger question, and one that cannot be neatly caught in a doctrine of *scriptural* authority alone.

Against this background, 'to take the Old Testament seriously' means both more and less than it is commonly supposed to mean. It does not mean holding any particular theory about the inspiration of these very words, or (as we shall see in the next chapter) the selection of precisely these books. It does not mean holding that any and every text in this corpus somehow has a Christological reference; nor, on the other hand, does it mean that the Old Testament Scriptures have authority for Christians irrespective of whether or not they are consistent with the fresh encounter with God mediated by Christ. It is, in that sense, less than what biblical conservatives mean by taking the Old Testament seriously. But on the other hand it does mean accepting the truth in Paul's completely non-polemical assumption that God was genuinely known in Israel before Christ came, and that the religion which already used these books as its frame of reference was a locus for a real encounter with the true God. It unquestionably entails some kind of theory about the providential character of the religion of Israel – part of which, of course, is the possession of the Law, the Prophets, and the Writings.

To a fundamentalist, this way of putting it sounds hopelessly vague and fuzzy at the edges. Any suggestion that divine providence requires *roughly* these books or *approximately* the religion of first-century Palestine as the matrix for Jesus provides an opportunity for sharpening up the thin end of the wedge: for once you start talking in such vague terms, where will you stop? Yet the claim being made is surely full of a particularity scandalous enough for any conservative. For we are saying, in effect, that we can have no doctrine of the authority of Scripture which is only a doctrine of the authority of Scripture; rather, we can account adequately for the position Scripture holds in the Christian faith only on the basis of a belief that God was genuinely and uniquely known in Israel, and was then made more perfectly known through Jesus Christ.

The reason why there seems superficially to be a contradiction between Paul's extreme claims for the newness of Christ and his unshakeable conviction that the old Scriptures remain valid, even self-evidently valid, is that our own frame of reference is too narrow. We think we are talking about the status of certain words on paper, and at that level there does seem to be a tension. Either the Old Testament is binding, or it is superseded. But Paul's framework is much wider. For him, Scripture is only part of the whole web of relationship between God and his people, and it is central to his gospel that this relationship is and remains a genuine one, though now (in Christ) greatly broadened and extended. 'The authority of the Old Testament' is a shorthand term for this belief in the truth of Israel's pre-Christian knowledge of God. It is only when its original context is lost that it comes to be taken overliterally, as the codification of a book rather than as loyalty to a living tradition of obedience to the living God, and of communion with him.

Only as we recapture a sense of distance from pre-Christian Israel – easier now than ever before in Christian history, thanks both to modern scholarship and to improved Jewish–Christian dialogue – can we resist the tendency to flatten out the books of the Old and New Testaments into a uniform 'Holy Scripture'; only then can we gain access to what was known of God before Jesus and, indeed, *by* Jesus. There is no road to knowing the Christian God which does not take seriously that he was and is also the God of the Jews, who spoke through prophets and sages who were not Christian, and who yet spoke truly; and who, in these last days, has spoken another word, by his Son our Lord Jesus Christ: the same word, yet not the same; a new word, yet one which does not annul the old.

Notes

1. On the questions discussed in this paragraph, see my 'Judaism and Christianity: Promise and Fulfilment', *Theology* 79 (1976), pp. 260–6.

2. Barnabas 6.11–12; tr. M. Staniforth, rev. A. Louth in *Early Christian Writings: The Apostolic Fathers* (London 1987), p. 166.

3. Clementine Recognitions 1.59; my translation.

4. H. von Campenhausen, *The Formation of the Christian Bible* (London 1972), p. 28.

5. Other examples are 1 Cor. 11.14–15; 14.7–11; 15.35–44; Gal. 3.2–5. Cf. O. Michel, *Paulus und seine Bibel* (Gütersloh 1929), p. 159.

6. von Campenhausen, *Formation*, p. 67.

7. Cf. Gal. 3.16; Rom. 4.3–17. See below, p. 28.

8. See M. F. Wiles, 'Scriptural Authority and Theological Construction: The Limitations of Narrative Interpretation', in G. Green, ed., *Scriptural Authority and Narrative Interpretation* (Philadelphia 1987), pp. 42–58; the term 'over-exegesis' occurs on p. 43.

9. See Jowett's famous essay 'On the Interpretation of Scripture', in *Essays and Reviews* (London 1860, ninth edn 1861), p. 368.

10. cf. J. Barr, *Holy Scripture: Canon, Authority, Criticism* (Philadelphia and Oxford 1983), p. 48: 'The pre-Christian basis of the church, though by shorthand we often call it the Old Testament, is in fact Israel. . .' Barr refers to the similar point made by H. Berkhof, *Christian Faith* (Grand Rapids 1979), p. 221: 'we are not concerned with the book as such, but with the faith and the history of the people of Israel to which this book bears witness'. The point is anticipated in a

letter sent by Walter Baumgartner to Karl Barth on 20 March 1940 ('Karl Barth und Walter Baumgartner: Ein Briefwechsel über das Alte Testament, herausgegeben von Rudolf Smend', *Zeitschrift für Theologie und Kirche* Beiheft 6 (*Zur Theologie Karl Barths. Beiträge aus Anlaß seines 100. Geburtstags*. Tübingen 1986), pp. 240–71; quotation from pp. 245–6; my translation): 'For you theological interest concentrates on, and is restricted to, the Bible *as a book* [das Bibel*buch*]. But just as in the case of the New Testament we move from the proclamation about Christ to the question about him as a real person, and about his life and its effect on others, so with the Old Testament: *behind* the Old Testament *the people of Israel* arises as the context within which the book originated.' As we shall see in the next chapter, many modern theologians share Barth's insistence that what lies *behind* the Bible is not theologically significant; but our argument clearly follows Baumgartner.

CHAPTER 3

The Question of the Canon

'All things necessary to salvation'

'The curse of the canon' sounds like the title of an ecclesiastical ghost-story. In reality, however, it is a phrase which (according to his former students) has often been used, though never committed to print, by Professor Christopher Evans, and it refers to the drawbacks for the Church of possessing a Bible which is officially limited to certain specified books. Scripture, as such, is not a 'curse'. But (according to Evans) it was a fateful day when the Church decided to rule a line under the last book to gain entry to the Bible, and to declare the canon of Scripture closed.[1] The word 'canon' is indeed traditionally used in Christianity in this narrowly defined sense, to denote a *closed and fixed list* of books, deemed to constitute the Scriptures. When Article 6 of the Thirty-Nine Articles of Religion of the Church of England declares that 'Holy Scripture containeth all things necessary to salvation', and then lists 'the names and number of the canonical books', it means 'canon' in this sense. It is not declaring that these books alone are good and useful, but that they constitute the *maximum* set of writings which can be appealed to as defining the Christian faith. The thrust of the Article is of course against Catholic claims about the authority of tradition alongside that of Scripture. In this context it means to say, not indeed that tradition is bad, but that it has no coercive force except in so far as Scripture supports it. Here the canon is a fixed list which declares that *only these* books are to be reckoned authoritative Scripture.

I

Now the concept of canon has been having what James Barr calls some adventures in modern theology,[2] of which there will be more to say shortly. But for the moment let us stay with this primary and traditional sense of the word. Though we have not described the canon as a curse, it could fairly be said that the thrust of our argument so far has been rather unfriendly to the idea of a fixed canon, at least so far as the Old Testament is concerned. Our quest for some primitive Christian opinions about the Jewish Scriptures has suggested, certainly, that Paul and his contemporaries accepted the Scriptures that had come down to them. But there is no reason to think that the first generation of Christians gave a moment's thought to exactly which books these were. One of the least plausible of all the ideas accepted by many fundamentalists is the notion that Jesus and his disciples had hard and fast views on which books ought to be reckoned scriptural. Neither Jesus nor Paul nor anyone else in the early Church, so far as we can tell, had any assumptions about this question that differed from their Jewish contemporaries. Like them they mostly took it for granted that the books that were read in the synagogue and quoted by teachers and scholars constituted 'the books', as Scripture was sometimes loosely known.

As is well known, New Testament writers at times cite books which would later be regarded by Jews and Christians alike as non-canonical, drawing no apparent distinction between them and the books now in our Bibles. Thus Jude 14 cites 1 Enoch 'with all the air of accepting it as a fully authoritative religious book . . . It is the fullest and most explicit use of an older sacred text within the letter.'[3] Paul seems to know and to have been influenced by the Wisdom of Solomon, which Catholics but not Protestants now count canonical.[4] Not only does the question of its canonicity not seem to interest or concern him, but it is not clear that it makes any conceivable difference to us whether we say that he thought it canonical or not, or whether we ourselves do so. None of the differences between Catholics and Protestants seems to relate in any way to the difference between their canons of the Old Testament. By relegating the 'apocryphal' books to an appendix the Church of England, like the other Protestant Churches, did nothing to change the content of the faith that was supposed to rest on the authority of Scripture.

This is why in the last chapter I happily spoke with deliberate vagueness of 'roughly these books' as the Bible to which Paul made sporadic reference in his epistles. In any case, as I tried to argue, it is only in a loose sense that 'the Bible' is Paul's source of authority at all. What matters to him is God's action in Christ, as related to God's previous actions or previous involvement with his people, and through them with the human race. The holy books of Judaism, whichever precisely those are, are the channel through which that past involvement is known in the present, and a continuing source of spiritual nourishment for the heirs of those with whom God made his covenant: they are not in themselves the one and only source of access to God.

The 'canon' of the New Testament is a much later development in any case. It was probably the absence of a New Testament that forced early Christian writers into much of the strained over-exegesis that passes for the argument from prophecy. If they had had an official Christian book, perhaps they would have felt less need to read the Old Testament as if *it* were a Christian book. Barnabas and 1 Clement are good examples of this: they feel the need of some normative document to which they can appeal in justification of Christian practices and beliefs, and since the old Scriptures are all they have, they are obliged to read Christian concerns into them. The sublime heights this can rise to are not to be scorned. No one can read Melito of Sardis' Paschal Homily – the early Christian commentary on the account of the Passover sacrifice in Exodus quoted at the end of the first chapter[5] – without seeing that profound insights resulted from this enforced pre-occupation with deriving Christian meanings from a non-Christian text. But it is doubtful whether Christianity could have sustained itself indefinitely without an official Scripture of its own. J. S. Semler, in his famous *Treatise on the free investigation of the canon*, thought it could: 'The basic teachings of Christianity were in themselves capable of being rightly and fully accepted, understood, and explained even without Scriptures and books.'[6] But perhaps if it had gone that way, and managed without a New Testament, it would also have had to abolish the Old Testament, or else the unsuitability of that collection on its own would have caused intolerable strains.

Even when a Christian canon did form, its *exact* limits mattered very little. There would certainly have been changes, subtle and not-so-subtle, in Christian belief, if particular books had been deliberately excluded or others that are now non-canonical included. But it is hard to say just what these changes would have been. For people do not as a matter of fact read the books that are there with an impartial eye, and then formulate their doctrines accordingly. They read the books that accord with their overall perception of the faith, and then read the others as if they said the same. This is not to imply that Christians simply read back later ideas into the Bible, but rather to note that certain parts of Scripture which are felt to be central tend to condition their reading of the rest. To take a small example: Paul tells us that 'sin came into the world through one man and death through sin' (Rom. 5.12). Consequently Christians always read Genesis 3 as if it said that Adam lost the gift of immortality, with which he was originally endowed, through his disobedience in the garden. Genesis appears to imply, however, that Adam was mortal anyway; it was *after* he ate the fruit that God feared he might be tempted to eat from the tree of life and so *become* immortal. Apparently he might well have done so, had God not expelled him from the garden and barred the way against his return.[7]

One effect of canonicity is thus to induce expectations of consistency with what one already perceives as the truth. This results in strained interpretations, in accordance with what we have called the principle of the 'semantic indeterminacy' of sacred texts.[8] It is only in modern times, and thanks to biblical criticism, that the conscious discipline of attending to the natural sense of biblical books rather than the sense that ecclesiastical tradition has attributed to them has made it possible for people to ask whether, for example, the Fourth Gospel may not be rather docetic, or the Pastoral Epistles rather stuffy and pedestrian. In the early Church, the attitude which would one day say, 'This book is in the canon, therefore we must make sure that its *distinctive* voice is heard in our formulations of the faith,' had not yet arrived.

II

Now this makes some of the 'adventures' of the canon in recent theology rather questionable. Once again, the difficulty is essentially that modern theological theories force us to make choices which early Christians did not have to make, while at the same time obscuring distinctions that were apparent to them. In recent theological writing, especially in America, there has been a conscious attempt to 'take the canon seriously'. We should recognize, it is argued, that the Church's decision to draw up a canon consisting of precisely these books, arranged in a particular order, should be a shaping influence on our understanding of the Christian faith. Here there is a subtle shift from a canon as a fixed list to 'canon' as an alternative name for 'Holy Scripture',[9] so that to say that the Bible is a canon means that it has authority *in its present form as a single book* – or, to use a modern literary technical term, as a 'work'. This is not just to say that the Bible has authority; it is to go well beyond this, and to say that its authority operates at the level of the finished form into which the Church has arranged it.

Thus in the work of B. S. Childs[10] the question is continually asked what *difference* is made to the meaning that a particular book or section of a book conveys by its canonical shaping: by the fact that it stands here rather than there in the canon, or that it is placed next to another book or section that may be said to modify its meaning. So, for example, the meaning of Psalm 1 or Psalm 150 is said to depend on the fact that they are the first and last psalms of the Psalter. To read them as if they were individual texts unrelated to the other psalms, though it may be interesting from a historical point of view, is not to read them *canonically* – that is, with the full meaning that the canonizing decision has imparted to them.

The idea of a 'canonical' meaning in this sense is a perfectly coherent one. It corresponds to the way many Christians have felt about the text of the Bible ever since – probably in the second or third century – the books of the Christian Bible were first combined between the covers of a single codex to form one volume in the modern sense. But 'canonization' in this extremely strong sense, the act by which 'the books' were turned into 'the Book', meant a large step, even if an often unrecognized one, from what was originally implied in drawing up a list of approved or accepted books. The consequent sense that the Bible is indeed a single book has introduced some anachronism into our percep-tions of what it meant to the very earliest Christians – living before such a one-volume Bible had been invented – to have a 'canon' of Scripture. To illustrate this, let us again sketch two positions which early Christians seem generally to have shared, yet which we would ourselves find it impossible to hold together. This will be the same approach that we followed in the first chapter to induce a sense of disorientation and so, perhaps, to help us break out of our modern assumptions.

On the one hand, then, we have to acknowledge that the authority of the books in the 'canon' was clearly much greater than it is for most modern people. This authority was felt to inhere in the exact verbal form of the biblical text to an extent now scarcely believed even by fundamentalists. Thus there is no sense in St Paul, for example, that the authority of the Scriptures lies in their general gist, or that it does not matter which words are used to express an idea. On the contrary, Paul often argues from precise details of the text, interpreting as significant features that actually lie below the level at which semantic significance is possible – words out of context, peculiarities of idiom, and so on. The stock example is his argument in Galatians 3.16 that God made his promises (in Genesis 15.5) to Abraham's 'seed' (singu-lar) not 'seeds' (plural), and that the promise therefore needs to have a single person (Christ, of course) as its fulfilment, rather than the whole Jewish people. Despite the labours of biblical conservatives to show that this is really a very reasonable argu-ment, and despite one's feeling that Paul was making a valid point even if he chose an unfortunate way to make it, the modern reader is bound to say that at the linguistic level at which it claims to operate the argument is simple nonsense. But such verbal quibbles are by no means uncommon in Paul or indeed in other early Christian writers, by whom the text is frequently tortured beyond what modern ideas about the semantic possibilities of texts will bear.[11]

But on the other hand, as we have already seen, the earliest Christians do not seem to have been in the least interested in the question just which books fell into the category of such inspired, holy Scripture. Any book that came their way and that seemed old and venerable, they were apt to treat as an authority in just the same way as the books we now call Scripture. In the world of the New Testament, Scripture was not 'a book', as in a modern (so-called) 'canonical' perspective, within which all sorts of structural relationships could be found; Scripture was a series of books or scrolls. Though it was clear that most of what we now call 'the Old Testament' was included in it, the sense that certain books were excluded was not very strong. The probability is that most Jewish communities possessed some rather than all of the scrolls of scriptural books. But when they *did* come into the possession of other books, including those that are not now regarded as canonical, they probably accorded them a similar status. Old books, in the Mediterranean world of the first century, tended to acquire a certain 'scriptural' or 'canonical' status merely because they were old, especially if they were like scriptural books in style, format and content. Even in the Christian community, when it began to 'canonize' its own sacred writings, it was a long time before all lists of holy books agreed, and even longer before books perceived as ancient or apostolic were positively rejected, even if they did not appear on an official list.

It is indeed hard for us, in a world of self-renewing libraries, to recapture the reverence with which people in many past cultures held old books. The respect of many medieval authors for the *auctores* of the past in fact greatly exceeded the respect which most modern Christians, if they are honest, could claim that they feel for the Bible. The drive to show that any proposition one wished to defend accorded with the teachings of at least some ancient authority was widespread throughout the ancient world. As Rudolf Bultmann showed long ago, when Paul cites a scriptural authority for some point he is making he is often doing no more than philosophical writers of his day, who liked to have an old opinion to quote in support of even the most banal remark.[12]

In this context, it is anachronistic to project back on to the period of Christian origins our sense that the canonization of the Bible sets it off from other books so much that it should be read as a single work with a unique character and strong internal cohesion. The canon of the New Testament or early patristic age is a *collection* of books, whose limits are not really clear, and which benefits from a general respect for the past unlike anything in modern intellectual culture. Both the Fathers and the New Testament writers themselves often quote from sacred books as 'the Scripture' (*hē graphē*), or introduce a quotation with the words 'as it is written'; but no discernible difference can be found between such references to books that we now reckon as Scripture and to other books. In just the same way *agrapha*, sayings of Jesus not now in any canonical Gospel, may not be frequent, but when they do occur, there is no apparent awareness that they are on a different level from 'scriptural' sayings.[13] Their authority is their dominical origin, not their inclusion in a 'canon'.

III

Thus, to summarize: 'Scripture' for the early Church was a much looser category than it is for us; yet its interpretation was often much more rigid. It seems to me that any satisfactory discussion of the canon or the canonical principle must do justice to both sides of this opposition, if it is not to be anachronistic. In my judgement modern 'canonical' approaches fail in this respect. But how can we account for this apparent contradiction, or what version of 'canonicity' will allow us to give full weight to both sides of it? The answer perhaps again lies in the direction of seeing that 'Scripture' or 'the Bible' serves well enough as a *rough* description of what it was that the early Church regarded as 'canonical', but that it fails when pressed (as it has been especially since the Reformation) as an exact and complete definition of the source of authority in the Christian religion. The books that are reckoned as holy Scripture are intimately related to the faith, indispensable for it, yet not conterminous with it. As Lessing pointed out two hundred years ago,[14] the Church in the first couple of centuries spoke more of the 'canon of truth' or the 'rule of faith' than of the canon of Scripture. This rather than Scripture itself was the ultimate 'canon' according to which all teaching had to be assessed. To quote von Campenhausen: 'The one rule and guideline, the only "canon" which Irenaeus explicitly acknowledges, is the "canon of truth", that is to say: the content of the faith itself, which the Church received from Christ, to which she remains faithful, and by which she lives.'[15] This is not to speak, as some counter-Reformation apologetic did, of an ecclesiastical tradition *additional* to the traditions in Scripture, containing extra dogmas, but of a framework within which both Scripture and church teaching must be heard and assimilated, and against which both may be judged.

This 'rule' or 'canon' provides a very basic outline of Christian doctrine, as we would now call it, and underlies rather than is identical with any particular formulations. For example, it is clear that the prefaces of Christian eucharistic prayers preserve in most traditions the rudiments of what Christians believe about the history of salvation. These prefaces tell a story running from creation through the history of Israel down to the work of Christ, and then on into the witness and Spirit-filled experience of the apostolic Church and the subsequent generations, up to and including the very congregation using the prayer in the present. They dictate how the history of both Old and New Testaments is to be read and interpreted. To quote the Liturgy of St John Chrysostom, it is to be read as an account of how God 'brought us into being out of nothingness, and when we fell away raised us up again, and does not cease till he has done everything necessary to bring us to the life of heaven and to confer on us the kingdom to come'. Such an account would rule out (for example) any reconstruction of the underlying 'plot' of the Old Testament histories in which the main characters were Cain, Jezebel and Nebuchadnezzar; or a reading of the New Testament as the history of a gnostic sect.

This is not to argue that acceptance of the rule of faith means that the modern Christian is *not allowed* to read the Bible except in ways sanctioned by this rule. It is simply to emphasize that, if we are speaking of *authority* for Christians, it lies with such a rule rather than with Scripture itself; for Scripture is capable of being read in many different ways. It is precisely because it is the rule of faith which determines or describes the basic contents of the faith that it does not matter so very much exactly which books are in the Bible and which are not. A completely different list would of course bring problems, but fuzziness at the edges is no problem at all. Disagreements about the canon, so long as they are not on a very large scale, do not matter much where there is a strong source of guidance on the contents of the faith from a rule or canon of faith. Within such a scheme of thought, what is assumed is not that all the books of Scripture cohere strongly in the sense that they form a single 'work', like a well-constructed novel by a single author, but that they are all written from within a genuine encounter with God. Their canonicity is not a fact about their internal structure or about their relationship with each other, but about their correspondence to an external norm, the faith of the Church.

Thus it does not seem very plausible to say that the Bible, 'as a canon', provides the framework (or even, as some now say, the *grammar*[16]) of Christian faith. The relationship is the other way around: the Christian faith provides the context within which the

Bible is read. The assertion that certain books deserve to be regarded as canonical is not a kind of performative utterance, asserting a decision to regard these books as the frame within which one will think. It is a thoroughly synthetic judgement, which declares that they have been found to speak of the God who is known in the Church's confession of faith.[17] Of course the faith and the Bible derive ultimately from the same source, the experience and thought of Israel and of the Church; but logical priority lies with the rule of faith.

Is this a Catholic theory of biblical authority? Well, in some ways it may seem so; though I should stress that we are talking not of the external or jurisdictional authority of the magisterium to define the faith, but of its inherent or internal authority, that which makes it compelling to the believer. This Catholicism, if such it is, is of a markedly Anglican variety! But in any case the argument will now take a turn which will, I hope, severely modify this 'Catholic' impression; for in the next chapter I shall turn to the question of how we judge the rule of faith itself, and here the Bible will make its entry once again as our major source of information and witness to the earliest Christian experience of God. I shall be arguing, however – and this is central – that the Bible does not exercise this role 'as Scripture' or 'as a canon' or 'as the grammar of faith', or whatever other formulation one may use, but as historical evidence: and that takes us a long way from the subject of the present chapter.

IV

Perhaps in conclusion we might find more to help us in another use of the term 'canon': the modern, secular literary use which derives from T. S. Eliot.[18] Eliot of course borrowed the term from theology, but he transformed it in the process. He spoke of the 'canon' of English literature, meaning those works which were acknowledged by all to constitute the essential corpus of classics.[19] (This idea has fallen on bad times in the literary world, but let that pass.[20]) He then argued that each new work which proved to be of classic stature itself at once entered into a relationship with the existing canon, a relationship of a subtle, reciprocal kind. Its meaning derived from the existing canon, for a work in a cultural vacuum would mean nothing at all. Rather, the existing works crowd round it and constrain the meanings it can bear. Yet, if it really is a classic, it has the power to change the canon, altering the relationships between the existing works and creating a new equilibrium in which every previous work takes on a new tinge of meaning.

Now 'canonical critics' do not seem to have used Eliot's ideas much, though one may surmise that the word 'canon' would not have sounded so self-evidently right (to American and British ears) as a description of the Bible, had ideas like Eliot's not been in the air. I certainly would not want to apply his scheme directly to the scriptural canon – partly because, as I have already indicated, I do not think that Scripture is a coherent corpus in the relevant sense: the principles on which the books in it were selected were certainly not literary ones. But if we are going to use the word 'canon' at all, we might do worse than apply Eliot's doctrine as an *analogy* or parable. We may use it to describe not the relationships among biblical books, but the relationship between the new faith, which is expressed in the 'canon of truth' or 'rule of faith', and the prior experience of God in Israel to which it has to be related.

The arrival of Jesus, and of the new work God has accomplished through him, draws its significance from the knowledge of God that already existed in Israel, and would be meaningless without it. Jesus' God is the God of Israel, and that means not only of ancient Israel, but of Judaism. Christians who are anti-semitic are cutting themselves off from their own roots, making Christianity into a new religion divorced from the God and Father of our Lord Jesus Christ, who is the God of the Jews. Yet at the same time, the whole structure of Israel's relationship with God is radically transformed and changed by what Eliot called 'the supervention of novelty'. This is not primarily a point about the meaning of texts: it is a matter of a new community, a new ethos, a new understanding of God – a new creation, Christians said. But it does have an effect on texts. It draws them into fresh conjunctions, destroys existing threads of connection, and establishes new ones. It is not purely accidental that Christians arrange their Old Testament differently from Jews, or that they came to set their own new Scriptures alongside the old ones and to present the two collections as at one and the same time in agreement and in tension with each other. Nor are they wrong to call the Old Testament 'old'; for not to do so is to deny that Christianity is really new. In this way the coming of Jesus, and the new community that resulted, has an effect on existing tradition – and that means also on existing Scripture – not unlike the effect of a new, classic work on a literary 'canon' in Eliot's sense.

Thus the literary use of the term 'canon' can be a useful tool to describe something very important about the Christian faith and its relation to the Judaism from which it sprang. But (and here we turn decisively towards the next chapter) this is an *analogy*. As James Barr puts it, 'Faith does not rest simply on texts, but also – and more – on persons and events. Faith stands or falls not with the status of a holy text – which was perhaps closer to the Jewish conception – but with the knowledge and meaning of these persons and events, which can be mediated by the text.'[21] Whether or not Judaism has become strictly the 'religion of a book', in the Qur'ānic sense, there can be little doubt that it is so in a more straightforward sense than Christianity. Christianity is not in the last resort about relations between texts, but about events in the real world: the Word of God did not for us become incarnate in a book, but in a life. The gospel is not about a new classification scheme for the religious library, but about new life in Christ.

Notes

1. Despite the absence of the actual phrase 'the curse of the canon' from C. F. Evans' published works, the line of argument it suggests can be found in his book *Is 'Holy Scripture' Christian? and Other Questions*, London 1971.

2. J. Barr, *Holy Scripture: Canon, Authority, Criticism* (Philadelphia and Oxford 1983), chapter 3 (pp. 47–74) is entitled 'The concept of canon and its modern adventures'.

3. J. Barr, *Escaping from Fundamentalism* (London 1984), pp. 42–3. Barr points out that in the same way Heb. 11.37 seems to refer to the *Martyrdom of Isaiah*. See also the detailed discussion of the Old Testament canon in my *Oracles of God: Perceptions of Ancient Prophecy in Israel after the Exile*, London 1986.

4. The discussion in Rom. 5 of the entry of death into the world through the sin of Adam (cf. p. 26) depends not on the 'canonical' version of the story of Adam and Eve in Gen. 3 but on a tradition found classically in Wisd. 2.23–4; cf. Barr, *Escaping*, pp. 44–5. The analysis in Rom. 1 of the gradual progress of sin in the history of mankind follows the outlines of the account in Wisd. 14: for a detailed comparison of the two texts see W. Sanday and A. C. Headlam, *A Critical and Exegetical Commentary on the Epistle to the Romans*, International Critical Commentary (Edinburgh 1895, fifth edn 1902), pp. 51–2.

5. cf. p. 10 above.

6. J. S. Semler, *Abhandlungen von einer freien Untersuchung des Canon* (Halle 1771–5), p. 99; my translation.

7. See above, note 2.

8. See above, p. 19.

9. See Barr, *Holy Scripture*, pp. 75–104.

10. See B. S. Childs, *Introduction to the Old Testament as Scripture*, Philadelphia and London 1979; *The New Testament as Canon: an Introduction*, Philadelphia and London 1984; *Old Testament Theology in a Canonical Context*, Philadelphia and London 1985. Childs' approach is often referred to as 'canonical criticism', though he himself dislikes this name: see my *Reading the Old Testament: Method in Biblical Study* (Philadelphia and London 1984), pp. 77–103 and 140–79. Cf. also D. H. Kelsey, *The Uses of Scripture in Recent Theology*, Philadelphia and London 1975, which often speaks of the use of the Bible in theology as a 'construal' of the text – rather as if it were a single sentence or paragraph.

11. The same passage from Gen. 15 is analysed in detail in Rom. 4, an extended

reflection on the implications of the word 'reckoned' in 15.6 ('Abraham believed God, and it was *reckoned* to him as righteousness').

12. R. Bultmann, *Der Stil der paulinischen Predigt und die kynisch-stoische Diatribe*, Göttingen 1910.

13. cf. A. C. Sundberg, art. 'Canon of the NT' in *The Interpreter's Dictionary of the Bible*, supplementary vol. (Nashville, Tenn., 1976), pp. 136–40.

14. G. E. Lessing, 'Necessary Answer to a Very Unnecessary Question of Herr Haupt-Pastor Goeze in Hamburg', in H. Chadwick, ed., *Lessing's Theological Writings. Selections in Translation with an Introductory Essay* (London 1956), p. 62: 'The content of the Creed is called by the earliest Fathers *regula fidei*. This *regula fidei* is not drawn from the writings of the New Testament. This *regula fidei* existed before a single book of the New Testament existed.'

15. H. von Campenhausen, *The Formation of the Christian Bible* (London 1972), p. 182.

16. cf. P. Holmer, *The Grammar of Faith*, New York 1978.

17. cf. O. O'Donovan, *On the Thirty-Nine Articles: A Conversation with Tudor Christianity* (Exeter 1986), p. 51: 'Scripture is authoritative precisely because of what it is and contains: within it "everlasting life is offered to men by Christ". It testifies in a decisive way to the historical event of the incarnation. Only on that ground can any book belong to the canon and count as Holy Scripture . . . In the final analysis, then, the New Testament has no authority which is not the authority of Jesus and the authority of the mighty acts of God involving him.' When O'Donovan goes on, however, to add the equal and opposite point that 'correspondingly, the authority of Jesus and of these events is (from an epistemological point of view) vested entirely in the New Testament, and communicated exclusively through its witness. There is no other route by which those events make themselves known to later generations,' I part company with him; see below, pp. 42–5.

18. cf. my article 'Judaism and Christianity: Promise and Fulfilment', *Theology* 79 (1976), pp. 260–6.

19. See T. S. Eliot, 'Tradition and the Individual Talent', in his *Selected Essays*, London 1932.

20. See F. Lentricchia, *After the New Criticism*, Chicago and London 1980; M. Butler, 'Revising the Canon', *Times Literary Supplement*, 4–10 December, 1987, pp. 1349–60.

21. J. Barr, 'Bibelkritik als theologische Aufklärung', in T. Rendtorff, ed., *Glaube und Toleranz: Das theologische Erbe der Aufklärung* (Gütersloh 1982), pp. 30–42; quotation from p. 41 (my translation).

CHAPTER 4

The Bible as Evidence

'These things are written, that you may believe'

Forty years ago Austin Farrer delivered his Bampton Lectures, published as *The Glass of Vision*.[1] They were a study of the nature of scriptural inspiration, which tried to show how God's revelation of himself is achieved through the controlling images of the Bible. If proof were needed that an entirely non-fundamentalist account of the Bible can still rest on an utter conviction of the supernatural character of Scripture, it would be hard to find any more luminous.

An essential feature of Farrer's treatment of the Bible was his belief that the place of Scripture in the Christian faith has to do primarily with our *knowledge* of God and his purposes for the world – that is, a doctrine of Scripture belongs to the epistemological portion of Christian theology. This is surely true, and important. Christians may well differ over the parts played respectively by natural and supernatural sources of knowledge in their faith, over the proper provinces of what is called natural and what is called revealed theology, over the relation of grace to nature in our understanding of God and his action in our world; and hence over how far the contents of the Bible should be seen as divinely inspired, and how far the product of the human religious quest. These questions have already concerned us, and will continue to do so. Nevertheless, Christians agree that there *are* certain truths which are entailed by the commitment to God in Christ into which they have entered. In Farrer's words, the Christian faith 'tells of the life of God in God, and it tells of divine purposes in the natural world transcending nature . . . And it says that in the created world there is a work of salvation, whereby mortal spirits are supernaturalized, and drawn into the participation of eternal being.'[2] But (he argues) if we claim to know, or to believe with good reason, that these things are so, we shall be hard put to it not to say that our knowledge or belief is connected in some way or other with the Bible. Whether or not in theory we can imagine the development of a Church holding such truths without the Bible, the Bible has in fact been the source of Christian faith down the centuries: and since that faith is a supernatural one, the Bible itself (he reasoned) must be seen as transcending nature, too, and hence as supernaturally inspired. It remained only to uncover the mechanism by which this inspiration operates, and this Farrer proceeded to do in the most sublime way.

I

Nevertheless, times have changed; and to say the same thing in the face of fresh questions may be to say something different. Even someone who could do justice to Farrer's genius might not want merely to repeat his thoughts today. It will not have gone unnoticed that so far in this book neither 'revelation' nor 'inspiration' has yet made more than a fleeting appearance. We have been able to say a lot about the status and place of the Bible without using either term. The suspicion this arouses is that we are treating the Bible 'merely as a human book'. The last chapter, with its comments on the fuzziness at the edges of the biblical canon, heightened this sense that there really is not a dividing line between the Word of God – the Scriptures – and the human words to be found in other writings: at most it is a matter of degree.

I doubt, in fact, whether 'revelation' and 'inspiration' are the best categories to use for understanding Scripture in any case. Neither ought now to have the same, almost self-evident, place in a theological account of Scripture that seemed natural in 1948. The idea inherent in them that Scripture conveys supernatural knowledge appears in many ways too simple an account of the complex interaction we have begun to uncover between the written text, the living faith and the savings events. The supernatural injection of revealed knowledge which is attributed to Scripture can, if we are not careful, make everything apart from itself unnecessary in the economy of salvation. As long as we have the Bible (it seems) Jesus need not really have existed, for it is the text that reveals the truth about God, not Jesus himself as he actually lived and died and rose again.

Farrer, of course, was far from believing that. His revelational view of Scripture was conceived as an apologetic remedy against the unbelief that he saw around him, especially in the philosophical atmosphere of post-war Oxford. He was right to see a rationalism wholly hostile to the Christian faith in the philosophy of his day, with logical positivism in the ascendant, but wrong (I believe) to see it also in biblical scholarship, which was much less unbelieving than he supposed. He saw the drive to read the Bible 'like any other book' as a liberal attack on the supernatural character of the Christian faith, a way of reducing it to easy religious platitudes. Times have changed indeed, and irrationalism rather than rationalism now seems (to me at least) to be the enemy of true religion. The religious world today is full of credulity and a seeking after six impossible things to believe before breakfast. For me the problem is not how to defend the supernatural character of the faith I profess, but how to connect it with knowledge in other fields, both scientific and humanistic. For that task an approach which fences off scriptural revelation from the rest of knowledge has its dangers.

Farrer's own system was one of infinite subtlety. What he took away from the cause of relating faith in God to the rest of knowledge, through what now seems perhaps an excessive concentration on revelation as the major category for understanding the Bible, he handsomely restored through his doctrine of double agency. In the epistemological sphere this implied that the supreme mode of revelation lay in the imperceptible operations of God on the natural structures of the mind.[3] Hence scriptural revelation operated not by suspending the normal operation of the poetic imagination, but by heightening it so that it became in the highest degree expressive of innate human capacities. If we *are* to speak of Scripture and the scriptural writers as conveying divine revelation, I do not think we shall see a more satisfying account than Farrer's.

But with less sophisticated handling a high doctrine of scriptural revelation can succeed only in insulating the Bible from other sources of knowledge. As already hinted in the last chapter, I fear this is happening in the movement now under way in America to treat the canon of Scripture as the irreducible framework within which all theological and religious discourse is obliged to take place. This produces what is now sometimes called a Wittgensteinian fideism applied to the text of the Bible.[4] As long as we are playing the religious language-game the Bible is wholly normative, and we cannot go beyond this book and ask critical questions about it. Is not this a kind of bibliolatry? But again, rather than attack it on a modern theological front, where I would be fighting rather far from home, I shall concentrate on comparing it with what I take to have been the function of Scripture in an earlier age, and see if there are currents of thought available there which can help us to a more balanced understanding for today.

II

If we approach the Bible with the expectation of finding infallible supernatural revelation in it, we are likely to be very puzzled by an early Christian writer such as Irenaeus, who has already been important in our discussion. As von Campenhausen shows particularly clearly, Irenaeus draws extensively on the New Testament to support his presentation of the faith, but (in this contrasting with his use of the Old Testament) he does *not* treat it as a divinely guaranteed source of supernatural information. He treats it as a reliable historical source.[5] Of course he does not have our ideas of what constitutes good historical source-material. Many of his judgements rest on a false belief that, for example, the Gospels were written by apostles or the friends of apostles, that the words of Jesus as there reported are his *ipsissima verba*, and so on. What he finds is really *testimony* in the ancient sense rather than evidence in the modern sense: friends you can trust, rather than sources you can torture.[6] In principle, however, this is still a long way removed from treating the New Testament as divine revelation.

This comes out particularly in the way he sifts its material into different piles which do not correspond with the present arrangement of the New Testament canon. Instead of treating the New Testament material simply as 'the Lord' and 'the Apostle' – that is, the Gospels and the epistles – as later writers generally do, Irenaeus works with a curious hybrid arrangement. He does treat the Gospels as one major source, but primarily as representing the testimony of the apostles who wrote them; and accordingly he treats the sayings of Jesus recorded in these same Gospels as a separate and independent category.[7] Lying behind this is a clear sense that the value of the Lord's own sayings for understanding and recognizing his divine authority does not depend on the fact that they appear in the pages of Christian holy books, but derives from the fact that Jesus actually said them. It is completely congruous with this that when Irenaeus cites *agrapha*, that is, sayings of Jesus preserved in the Church's oral tradition but not now appearing in any Gospel, he treats them as of completely equal authority and status with 'canonical' sayings.[8]

The authority of the Gospels, similarly, is treated as being the authority of the apostles who are supposed to have written them; it is as these men's testimony, not as holy Scripture, that the Gospels are to be believed. The Gospels are holy only because and in so far as they preserve what the Lord actually said and did, and what his first followers said and believed about him; they are not in the modern, strong sense of the term, a 'canon'. Irenaeus admittedly does not apply the same methods to the Old Testament, which he treats much more unequivocally as 'Scripture'. But even there he is interested in what can be learnt from its pages of the history of Israel and of God's dealings with his people. He does not show much tendency to regard the Old Testament as oracular in character. No doubt his strong sense of salvation-history is a factor here in ruling out a reading of the Old Testament as a collection of timeless truths: his use of it contrasts very sharply with, say, Origen's much less historical approach.

On the basis of Irenaeus one can thus make out a good case for treating the whole Bible (Old as well as New Testament) more as a collection of documents providing the evidence to which Christian faith in the present has to do justice, than as a self-contained body of supernatural revelation. This does not in any way detract from Irenaeus' sense that we should not have these books without divine providence, and nor need it from ours. But it does mark out a function for them which is some distance removed from the function they have in a conservative biblicism.

The Bible matters, to put it at its simplest, because it is the earliest and most compelling evidence that Jesus rose from the dead, and that he was such a person that his rising from the dead is gospel, good news. For some modern biblicism, both in its fundamentalist variety and in the immensely more sophisticated version we find in some modern hermeneutical movements, one could almost believe that Jesus rose from the dead in order to legitimate the Bible. Many who reacted in anger to the Bishop of Durham's remarks about the empty tomb in 1985 were not, I believe, interested in what he had to say about the resurrection as such, but much more with the fact that he was contradicting statements made in the New Testament.[9] That, rather than any doctrinal question, was what worried them. The fact that it was the resurrection about which historical questions were being raised was really a side-issue, for from such a perspective the resurrection is really no more important than any other event recorded in Scripture; it is the factual accuracy of Scripture as such that matters. It is at this point that one begins to see why some people would describe fundamentalism as a heresy – that is, a kind of single-issue fanaticism which destroys the structure of the Christian faith. I do not believe any good is done by bandying about words like 'heresy' in the modern Church; but the substantive point being made here is an important one.

II

But I had better turn from attacking others to the defence of my own position, which may well seem just as unsatisfactory. It will be said, no doubt, that the position I have adopted is a historicist one, even (perish the thought) a positivist-historicist one. First, it reduces the New Testament to the status of a collection of histori-

The Bible as Evidence

cal 'hard facts'; second, it puts Christian faith at the mercy of historical-critical scholars, a notoriously untrustworthy bunch; and third, it removes the *authority* of the Bible altogether, making it no more than a few rather ordinary old texts.

I reply to the first of these charges, that the New Testament is indeed historical evidence, but that does not mean it is evidence only for events or 'facts'. It is also evidence for the beliefs of the first Christians and for their reaction to the events on which Christian faith rests. To the second charge, that this is to make Christianity vulnerable to historical enquiry, I would say that the alternative – the attempt to place it above contradiction by historians – is simply to make it vacuous, and my withers are entirely unwrung by churchmen who say that this is to place the Church under the tyranny of the (supposedly notoriously inconsistent) guild of professional biblical scholars. Whatever may be true in other Churches or in other countries, the Church of England could hardly be said to pay excessive attention to its biblical specialists; the Anglican faithful do not tremble at the opinions of professors.

But to the third charge, that by seeing the Bible primarily as evidence we reduce its authority to something unworthily and merely human, I would reply like Paul, 'Do we hereby abolish the authority of the Bible? No, we establish it.' For the recognition that the Bible is primarily of value as evidence is a way of reasserting the authority of the Bible over the contents of Christian tradition. As a 'holy book' the Bible cannot, as we saw in the last chapter, control the rule of faith; it is the rule of faith that controls how we read the Bible. The Bible is too baggy and amorphous, and its interpretation is too uncertain if it is read as a single work, for it to determine the shape of the Christian faith. Opening a Bible for the first time, one could only repeat the reply of the Ethiopian eunuch when Philip asked him, 'Do you understand what you are reading?': 'How can I, unless some one guides me?' (Acts 8.30–1). As a guide to faith the canon of Scripture, accepted as equally authoritative in all its parts, is useless. But *once given* the Church's rule of faith, the books of the Bible exercise an extremely powerful check on that rule by providing a record of the roots of the Judaeo-Christian tradition. This record, being fixed in writing, cannot change, and the authenticity of what the Church at any given moment is making of the Christian faith can therefore be checked against it. Paradoxically, it is precisely too high a view of scriptural inspiration that would detach the Bible from its historical moorings and allow it to float freely in a timeless realm, thereby making it unable to exist 'back there', at the beginning of the tradition, and so to witness to the tradition's roots.

41

If we consider the ways in which the Bible, once seen as a set of documents with a specific context in the life of ancient Israel and of the early Church, can act as a check and control on modern expressions of Christian faith, then we shall see through the other two objections: that this is to treat it with merely 'historicist' concerns, and that it is to subject it to the authority of the professors, rather than of the Church or the believer. These objections fail, in two ways, to do justice to the realities of the relation between Scripture and doctrine.

First, it is true that one of the areas in which the Bible provides us with evidence is the realm of historical events. The Bible, certainly, is largely a document of faith, in which certain events are recorded not to provide material for historical curiosity but 'that you may believe'. But it does not at all follow from this that we are obliged either to accept or reject the whole of the Bible's presentation of history as a package deal, and that it is illegitimate to ask questions about its historical accuracy. When the Fourth Gospel tells us that 'these things are written, that you may believe' (John 20.30–1), it means precisely those things which it attests as having actually happened, in a terribly naive and every-day sense of those words – hence the appeal to eyewitness confirmation. Now for us the fact that it is hard to believe that some of the events in the Gospels – perhaps especially in the Fourth Gospel – actually did happen is a problem, and no amount of hermeneutical sophistication can eliminate the problem. If enough of the events reported in the Gospels really did seem to be fictions, there would come a point when we should responsibly have to ask whether the Christian faith was still believable. As James Barr says, 'Few would be willing to rest content with a Jesus who in historical fact was an unprincipled crook, a used-chariot salesman of the time.'[10] Probably this kind of argument applies to far fewer of the events recorded in the Gospels than people at large think, but the quantitative point must not be allowed to obscure the qualitative: what Jesus actually was and did is important for Christian faith.

I am aware that within the theological world this does indeed sound terribly naive, and that I seem to be talking like a survivor from the time before David Friedrich Strauss wrote his *Life of Jesus Critically Examined*[11] – indeed, before Lessing's assertion that there is 'an ugly, broad ditch' between 'accidental truths of history' and 'necessary truths of reason'.[12] To me, one of the strangest aspects of the modern theological scene is that very conservative Christians have decided to throw in their lot with Lessing and his heirs. An older biblical conservatism was more inclined to think that the truths of the gospel were *not* 'necessary

truths of reason', but contingent historical facts. This seems to me
a much sounder point of view. It is precisely because I am at one
with conservatives of that kind that I cannot share a desire to
place the Gospels above historical enquiry. A historical truth
which is not vulnerable to historical science is not a historical
truth at all.

The *authority* of the New Testament for modern believers is
not that it enables them to be supernaturally sure of alleged
events which they would otherwise entertain well-founded
doubts about. On the contrary, the New Testament is authoritative because it provides at least some of the early evidence with
which it is possible to judge how far the Christian faith really
does have a secure historical foundation. This is not to say that
historical knowledge is a *sufficient* basis for faith. German
theologians are right to regard the extreme kind of appeal to
'evidences' that once characterized English Christianity as
compromising the principle of justification by faith alone, and as
representing a desire to have God taped. But no one supposes
that historical study can provide a *sufficient* ground for faith.
What it can undoubtedly do, however, is to provide a check on
faith: is what Christians assert about Jesus, or about the activity
of God in Israel, compatible with what can be historically
known? Christianity is unusual among the world's great
religions in possessing so many very early documents about its
founder. The Reformation appeal to Scripture against tradition,
by which nothing is required to be believed as necessary to
salvation if it cannot be proved by certain warrants of Scripture,
corresponds to something that Irenaeus certainly believed:
namely, that Christianity would stand up only if it could be
shown to rest on authentic documentation. Modern historical
study of the Gospels warrants the same interpretation. It is
nonsense to think that the results of historical study have no
bearing on the Christian faith, as though the Bible existed in a
world out of the reach of historical enquiry. The attempt to place
it there, so far from according with its status and authority,
actually empties it of the very kind of authority that early
apologists like Irenaeus claimed for it: its character as early
evidence. The last years have seen an unprecedented flowering
of historical study of the New Testament by both Christian and
Jewish scholars; it will be a tragedy if theologians find specious
reasons of theological principle by which to claim that all this
work makes no difference.[13]

But secondly, the Bible is not only evidence for events; it is
also, and more obviously, evidence for the faith of Israel and of
the early Church. It thus continues to stand as a fixed norm

against which doctrinal affirmations can be tested, not indeed for truth, but for authenticity. The question whether a given doctrine is *true* cannot be resolved merely by saying that it is consistent with the witness of Scripture: by now no one will suspect that I believe that to be so. The testing of doctrinal formulations requires us to refer them to criteria of coherence and validity which theology shares in principle with other disciplines, and this is a complex process. Reference to 'what Scripture teaches' will not resolve it simply. But that does not mean that no reference to Scripture is required at all. What a comparison of our formulations with the biblical witness can do is to show us how far they accord with the faith of our first Christian ancestors. By retaining their expression of it as an official text, we assert that Christianity is not just whatever Christians happen to believe at a given moment, a continuously developing corpus of belief with no fixed points, but (in one important sense of an overworked phrase) a historical religion with roots in quite specific events in a particular period.

Thus again it is not the Bible as a single text or 'work' which is normative for faith, as a kind of literary classic from the Christian past, but the Bible as a collection of pieces of very early evidence of what Christians first believed; or (let us say rather) of the *gospel* as it was first heard by Christians. Note that this again argues for a certain looseness about the canon. That the New Testament contains our earliest witnesses is a fact which is perfectly contingent – if indeed it is a fact at all. If, as some think, the work known as the *Didache* or Teaching of the Twelve Apostles is older than some of the New Testament epistles, then from this perspective it too has a role to play in keeping Christianity in touch with its roots.[14] In theory we have to admit the possibility that some very old document could turn up that would seriously modify our impression of what the first Christians believed. Christianity remains vulnerable to this kind of discovery. The religious mind has a great craving for infallible knowledge, and would like the Christian foundation documents to be miles above even possible contradiction. But I think one can be quite secure in possession of what one believes to be the truth, without needing a Pope, either of flesh and blood or of paper and ink, to make assurance doubly sure. Truth plain and simple is better, in the mind of this Anglican at least, than infallibility. Austin Farrer put this point with the utmost clarity:

> It is my special concern, as a reformed Christian, to emphasize the necessity of a constant overhaul of dogmatic development by the standard of Christian origins; and 'Christian origins' can only mean in practice the *evidences we have* for

Christian origins . . . What I have to point out is that to admit primitivity as a judge or as a control is to submit to scholarship or historianship; and the scholar or historian is fallible; his work is endlessly corrigible, or subject to revision . . . I realize, of course, that my main contention . . . wears superficially the face of paradox. For what am I saying? That Christian developments must be anchored to Christian origins, and that the anchor-chains will only be strong if the links composing them are weak – the links of infallible authority would be less effective in binding us to our origins, than would the most fallible procedures of historical science. But if there is a paradox here, it is a paradox which the modern world is happy to swallow every day for breakfast, lunch and dinner. Until some time in the early eighteenth century it was commonly supposed that the truth of nature could not be effectively binding on our minds unless it informed us through infallible reasonings derived from incontestable axioms. We have now most thoroughly repented of any such belief. By admitting the purely provisional and wholly corrigible character of our physical investigations we have learnt how to expose ourselves to the truth. It is a matter of choosing between appropriate procedures admitted fallible and pretended infallible procedures proved inappropriate.[15]

III

The authority of the Bible for faith is thus not to be conceived of after the model of a code or textbook to which we can appeal to guarantee the truth of our beliefs, but after the analogy of a trusted friend, on whose impressions and interpretations of an important event or experience we place reliance. To put the matter rather differently, in terms that perhaps come more easily to an Old Testament specialist: the Bible is not a collection of divine oracles or directives, words uttered by God to which adherence must be given and which we must find some way, by hook or by crook, of translating into human language. The Bible in any case speaks, as the Jewish tag has it, 'according to the tongue of the sons of men': it is the words of human beings, mostly more like what biblical scholars call *wisdom* literature than oracular divine utterances. Few passages indeed in the Bible are actually said, in context, to be utterances of God: the prophetic 'Thus says the LORD' is the exception rather than the rule, a fact which works on scriptural inspiration seem sometimes to overlook. Even C. H. Dodd's great book *The Authority of the Bible*[16] begins from the prophetic paradigm, and thereby, I think, gets off on the wrong foot. The Bible is human reflection on the mystery of God, sparked off indeed by the fresh divine input into the human situation, in ancient Israel and in the first-century Mediterranean world through Jesus and his first disciples, but still remaining through and through a human book. This literature is not of divine origin; but for all that it has proved itself to be truly 'wisdom', the means whereby the gospel can continue to be preached and heard. It is not as a holy text, but as a unique witness to this gospel that the Bible has authority for the Christian. We do it less than justice if we set it on a pedestal that it does not need.

Notes

1. A. M. Farrer, *The Glass of Vision*, London 1948.

2. ibid., p. 31.

3. See especially *A Science of God?* London 1966 (= *God is Not Dead*, New York 1966), and cf. also *The Freedom of the Will* (London 1958), esp. pp. 297–315, and *Faith and Speculation* (London 1967), pp. 52–67.

4. See the discussion of this in G. Green, '"The Bible as . . .": Fictional Narrative and Scriptural Truth', in G. Green, ed., *Scriptural Authority and Narrative Interpretation* (Philadelphia 1987), pp. 79–96; cf. also M. F. Wiles, 'The Reasonableness of Christianity', in W. J. Abraham and S.W. Holtzer, eds, *The Rationality of Religious Belief. Essays in Honour of Basil Mitchell* (Oxford 1987), pp. 39–51, especially pp. 42–3.

5. See H. von Campenhausen, *The Formation of the Christian Bible* (London 1972), pp. 181–91; 'Marcion et les origines du canon néotestamentaire', *Revue d'histoire et de philosophie religieuses* 46 (1966), pp. 213–26, esp. pp. 225–6.

6. For this distinction see J. L. Houlden, *Connections: The Integration of Theology and Faith* (London 1986), pp. 36, 139–53, and p. 185, note 16, referring to *A Third Collection: Papers by Bernard J. F. Lonergan SJ* (London 1985), p. 80.

7. See Irenaeus *adversus haereses* ii.35.4; iii.11.9; iii.25.7; iv.praef.1; iv.41.4–6; v.praef. Cf. von Campenhausen, *Formation*, p. 191.

8. cf. chapter 3, note 13, above (p.35).

9. See D. Holloway, *The Church of England: Where is it going?* (Eastbourne 1985), esp. pp. 11–21, 46–69.

10. J. Barr, 'Exegesis as a Theological Discipline Reconsidered and the Shadow of the Jesus of History', in *The Hermeneutical Quest. Essays in Honor of James Luther Mays on his Sixty-Fifth Birthday* (Allison Park, Penn., 1986), pp. 11–45; quotation on p. 35.

11. D. F. Strauss, *The Life of Jesus Critically Examined* (1835), English tr. 1846, repr. London 1973. Strauss reconstructed a Jesus radically different from the figure in whom Christians have traditionally believed, but went on to argue that the discrepancy did not matter, because the 'historical Jesus' was not important for faith in any case.

12. G. E. Lessing, 'On the Proof of the Spirit and of Power', in H. Chadwick, ed., *Lessing's Theological Writings. Selections in Translation with an Introductory Essay* (London 1956), pp. 51–6.

13. In recent years the dismissal of any interest in reconstructing the history underlying the New Testament as 'historicist' or 'positivist' has received a fresh impetus from the vogue for 'narrative theology', which emphasizes that it is the *story* the Bible tells, not the history that lies behind it, that matters for faith. The desirability of a narrative theology was demonstrated with great acumen by H. W. Frei in *The Eclipse of Biblical Narrative: A Study in Eighteenth and Nineteenth Century Hermeneutics* (New Haven 1974). Frei is far from indifferent to reconstructive historical research, but the movement that takes its rise from him has tended towards a fideistic acceptance of the biblical narrative. It has discouraged historical research into the underlying events by appealing to principles like those enunciated by Lessing. See, for example, R. E. Thiemann, *Revelation and Theology: The Gospel as Narrated Promise*, Notre Dame 1985, and C. M. Wood, *The Formation of Christian Understanding: An Essay in Theological Hermeneutics*, Philadelphia 1981. There is a critical discussion of these movements in M. F. Wiles, 'Scriptural Authority and Theological Construction: The Limitations of Narrative Interpretation', in G. Green, ed., *Scriptural Authority and Narrative Interpretation* (Philadelphia 1987), pp. 42–58, and K. Stendahl, 'The Bible as a Classic and the Bible as Holy Scripture', *Journal of Biblical Literature* 103 (1984), pp. 3–10. An important stimulus to 'narrative theology' has been Karl Barth's anti-liberal opposition to 'historicism' in biblical criticism: 'Theology . . . ought to . . . resist this temptation, to leave the curious question of what is perhaps behind the texts, and to turn with all the more attentiveness, accuracy and love to the texts as such' (*Church Dogmatics* I/2 (Edinburgh 1956), pp. 493–4; cf. IV/2 (Edinburgh 1958), pp. 478–9). Cf. the discussion of Barth in D. H. Kelsey, *The Uses of Scripture in Recent Theology* (Philadelphia 1975), pp. 39–50, and the comments above in chapter 2, note 10 (pp. 22–3).

14. See the brief discussion of this vexed issue by A. Louth in *Early Christian Writings: The Apostolic Fathers* (London 1987), pp. 187–90.

15. A. M. Farrer, 'Infallibility and Historical Revelation', in M. D. Goulder, ed., *Infallibility in the Church: An Anglican-Catholic Dialogue* (London 1968), pp. 9–23; quotation on pp. 17–18.

16. C. H. Dodd, *The Authority of the Bible*, London 1929. The expression 'the prophetic paradigm' comes from J. Barr, *Escaping from Fundamentalism* (London 1984), p. 20. Christians seldom notice how little of the contents of the Bible are said, in the text itself, to be given by God. The problem was noticed by Jewish groups in New Testament times, however, who produced rewritten versions of biblical books in which 'dictation' by God or an angel was strongly affirmed – the Book of Jubilees is an outstanding example.

CHAPTER 5

The Bible as Theology

'From faith to faith'

The general drift of our discussion so far has been to open up a space between the Scriptures and the Christian faith. Most of our problems about biblical authority stem, we have argued, from too close an identification between the two. Either Scripture is assumed to teach identically the same as the Church in its confession of faith, with the result that the straightforward meaning of the biblical text has to be falsified in order to read into it the message the Church wants to hear; or else the faith is regarded as a summary of what is in Scripture, so that every portion of Scripture is capable of dictating what Christians should think or do. This produces an equal and opposite distortion: a religious system that can rightly be called 'legalistic', and which touches the gospel of God's redeeming love in Christ at best tangentially. Fundamentalist religion, I am sorry to say, exemplifies *both* tendencies at the same time. In it we find a legalistic adherence to what are called 'scriptural' doctrines, that is, doctrines derived from the Bible as from a textbook. Yet at the same time there is often a recourse to allegorical or strained exegesis wherever the natural sense of the text conflicts with cherished evangelical beliefs or practices – or indeed with scientific truth which fundamentalists, for all their vaunted rejection of post-Enlightenment culture, are too modern to deny.

But fundamentalism is only the limiting case of a problem inherent in any close identification of the Bible and the Christian faith. It would be quite unfair to think that biblical conservatives were uniquely affected by this problem, still more unfair to suppose that they were uniquely to blame for it. It is a problem for Protestantism in general. By putting a space between the two, I have been arguing, we do not by any means reduce the Bible's status, for we become able to read it far more on its own terms and thus more justly, and we are free to allow it its proper authority. We made a start on spelling out where that authority lies by speaking of the Bible as *evidence*. It is indeed the primary evidence for the great events from which Christian faith derives, and which remain its essential bedrock. Sophisticated trends in modern theology claim that it is the events as believed and preached rather than the 'bare' events as they happened that matter for faith, and this is true so far as it goes. But the point must not be pressed so far as to make the actual occurrence or otherwise of these events a matter of indifference: that is a theologians' exaggeration. As James Barr puts it, 'there is no question that Jesus "canonically" rose from the dead, but it is the extrinsic resurrection that matters for faith'.[1]

At the same time, of course, there are exceedingly few *events* recorded in Scripture which are crucial in that sense to Christian faith. The Bible is historical evidence in a much wider sense than this; evidence not simply for particular events, but for the whole world into which Jesus came. And though this does have to do with the chains of events that went to form his social setting and historical context, Scripture is most importantly a witness to the belief systems of Judaism and early Christianity, within which alone his meaning and role can be understood. This does not mean that it is a 'witness' in a theological or (as we might say) supernatural sense, but that it is a witness in the normal historian's sense: primary evidence from the periods about which we need to be informed. As we noted in the last chapter, this means that the Bible is not unique in principle – other equally early evidence could exist and may exist; but that it is more or less unique in practice can scarcely be doubted. It is its evidential value in this sense that is often stressed by early Christian writers. Though they usually lacked the necessary historical skill to evaluate the evidence and so get beneath the surface of the Bible, their instinct was a true one. In saying all this I am not trying to sell theology to a positivistic historicism. The easy equation of all interest in historical detail with an unreconstructed historic*ism*, which is sometimes falsely believed to have characterized mainstream biblical criticism in the past, is I believe one of the most unfortunate false trails in modern theology.

Nevertheless, to say that the Bible is historical evidence is *only* a beginning of a definition of its authority within Christianity. It remains true, after all, that the Bible is a book of faith. As John 20.31 puts it, 'these [things] are written that you may believe', not 'that you may have access to historical information'. The Bible is above all a theological, rather than a historical, book: the codified remains not of all the literature of ancient Israel and the early Church, but of their religious literature. If the first element in any theory of biblical authority needs to be the Bible as historical evidence, the second should be the Bible as theological or religious evidence. And so in this chapter we shall try to explore what might be meant by saying that the Bible speaks 'from faith to faith'.

I

To call the Bible theological evidence is to say that Christians can appeal to it for insight into the nature and purposes of God. D. H. Kelsey, in his *The Uses of Scripture in Recent Theology*,[2] introduced the word 'authorize' as a technical term for the way the Bible functions in respect of theological statements or systems. The Bible is said to 'authorize' this or that theological assertion, when people cite some part of the Bible to justify or reinforce it. Authorization, in this sense, can range from the crudest proof-texting – as if we were to write, 'God made the world, cf. Genesis 1.1' – to the most sophisticated biblical theologies, where an entire theological system is presented as an unpacking of the religious truth enshrined in the Bible. Kelsey's own book is full of intricate analyses of the different levels at which various theologians have used the Bible to 'authorize' their theologies. Probably much useful work could be done along these lines, especially as there is often a wide difference between the theory of biblical authority to which theologians are explicitly committed and the use they make of the Bible in practice. In this chapter, however, I propose to forgo a survey of the many and various things that can go wrong with the biblical authorization of theology, and to concentrate on a theologian who seems to me to show how it can go right. The theologian is Gerd Theissen, and the book I want to discuss is the aptly named *Biblical Faith*.[3] Its subtitle, *An Evolutionary Approach*, identifies what it is that is being, in Kelsey's terms, 'authorized' from the Bible. I must sketch Theissen's thesis briefly, before trying to show how he uses the Bible and what, if he is right, must follow for our ideas of biblical authority.

The case Theissen argues is a complex one, in which the coming of Jesus and of the distinctive style of faith which characterizes his disciples is seen as a fresh stage in human evolution. Unlike the now rather unpopular theories of Teilhard de Chardin, which attempted to understand Christ as a step on the path to the 'one far-off divine event to which the whole creation moves',[4] Theissen's work has no developed teleological aim. He believes fully in random selection. But he argues that from time to time the human race shows itself capable of what he calls an 'evolution against evolution'. At such moments the inherent selfishness of genetic and biological development (as described, for instance, by Richard Dawkins in *The Selfish Gene*[5]) goes mysteriously into reverse, and altruism arises. Altruism is a move against selection and towards the protection, instead of the destruction and elimination, of the weak.

Now Theissen maintains that we can see this happening in two highly distinctive phases of human religious history: in the increasingly monotheistic faith of ancient Israel, and in the life, teaching and death of Jesus of Nazareth. In an evolutionary perspective religion has often been simply one of the social mechanisms by which control, and hence the continued survival of the strong, is established; but in these two cases religion takes an unprecedented turn, and becomes instead an agency of healing for the wounded. In the religion of the prophets, and in the religious commitment for which Jesus lived and died, we see the distillation of faith in a God who is on the side of the downtrodden rather than of their oppressors, and who seeks to bring a new, supernatural order of justice and peace out of the natural laws of selection and mutation that spell death for the weak and powerless.

To do justice to Theissen's thesis and to tease out its implications for biblical authority it will be necessary to begin with some extensive quotation from his book.

> The thesis of this book is that if culture generally is a process which reduces selection, religion is the heart of human culture. It is a rebellion against the principle of selection. It makes human beings open to a greater reality before which each individual has infinite value . . . Experiences with this reality are gathered together in exemplary form in the Bible. It is probable that they are had everywhere. However, it seems to me that nowhere does the rebellion against the principle of selection emerge more clearly than in belief in the one and only God who brought Israel out of Egypt, who revealed himself in Jesus of Nazareth and continues to be accessible to humanity in the experience of the Spirit. (*Biblical Faith*, pp. 49–50)
>
> In an evolutionary perspective, the prophetic breakthrough to belief in the one and only God can be regarded as a 'mutation' of our religious life, a successful mutation, if we accept that it has led to a more adequate adaptation to the ultimate reality. This adaptation is not limited to the theoretical conviction that there is only one God, a conviction at which the Greek philosophers also arrived. Its practical aspect is also decisive. Faith in this one God means conversion and a change of behaviour. Because God is wholly other, he calls for a change in human behaviour.
>
> Now Christian faith says that this God has finally revealed himself in Jesus Christ. In the midst of human history there has been a valid demonstration of the necessary direction any change of behaviour has to take if it is to correspond to the ultimate reality. In the midst of history a possible 'goal' of evolution is revealed: complete adaptation to the reality of God. (p. 83)

Every page in the New Testament expresses the conviction that a fundamentally new form of humanity has appeared which exceeds all previous human possibilities. A 'mutation' has taken place. The new feature is love. This is not to be understood, subjectively, as an emotional bond, which is the way we usually interpret it, but as solidarity with the weak, a contradiction of the processes in nature and history which are oriented on selection. In this love God reveals himself. (p. 87)

Primitive Christian faith expresses its protest against selection most clearly in belief in the resurrection of the crucified Jesus. Here a helpless man is proclaimed ruler of the world, the sacrifice is proclaimed the priest, the condemned man is proclaimed the judge and the outcast the focal point of society. What was rejected by death as dysfunctional in the process of selection here becomes the starting point for a new development and the basis for unconditional motivation to live. (pp. 118–19)

Now we are not primarily concerned here with whether or not Theissen's overall case is correct – though it will be clear from the way I have described it that I think it is, and find it profoundly illuminating. Our concern is rather to ask, 'In what sense is the style of faith Theissen describes properly called, as it is in his title, biblical faith?' Obviously, in establishing this thesis Theissen is heavily dependent on the Bible, since the Bible provides most of what we know about ancient Israel and about Jesus of Nazareth and his first followers. Equally, however, 'biblical faith' cannot mean the system of belief that can be extracted from the Bible read ('canonically') as a single and self-consistent text. Theissen shows how, for example, parts of the New Testament reflect compromises which undermine aspects of the faith Jesus stood for, by insisting on rigid structures of church authority; and how there are strains of thought within the Old Testament which deny the cause of the poor and helpless, against the teaching of the prophets. Neither Judaism nor Christianity as they have in fact developed has been true at all points to what Theissen calls 'biblical faith'. Indeed, by establishing the canon of just these books as their holy Scriptures both religions ensured that alternative voices would continue to be heard in church and synagogue – voices belonging much more to religion in the bad old sense as an epiphenomenon of the human drive for social control and successful aggression, than to pure 'biblical faith'.

So if we are to understand why Theissen calls the development he describes 'biblical faith', we must take him to mean something like a style of faith to which the Bible gives us access, rather than one to which it unequivocally witnesses in all its parts. Biblical faith is the faith we encounter especially in the Bible, even only in the Bible, but not a religion that takes the Bible as its primary datum or which can be found evenly distributed throughout the Bible.

So long in fact as we insist on regarding the Bible as a book, a collection of texts, the 'canon', we can only understand Theissen by arguing that he wants there to be a 'canon within the canon' – that Lutheran expression so detested by Anglo-Saxon theologians. Of course this canon will turn out to consist principally of the books of the prophets and the major epistles of St Paul; for of the Lutheran provenance of Theissen's thesis there can be no doubt. We cannot understand him except as implying the need for a canon within the canon, if our own vantage-point is a high biblicism; and from that vantage-point we shall find ourselves having to ask how biblicism has to be modified to accommodate his position. But this is not the best or most natural way of understanding what he is trying to do. Central to his theory is a proposal not about the authority or integrity of the Bible as a literary document, but about the implication and meaning of developments that took place in the real world: insights arrived at and expressed in the lives and lifestyles of people who actually lived and died. Anyone with a taste for calling Christianity a historical religion, or for affirming the 'scandal of particularity', need look no further than *Biblical Faith*. It is not talking about possible theological doctrines which one can find in particular texts, but about what actually happened in ancient Israel and in the life and death of Jesus and in the establishment of the Christian Church. The 'canon', if we are to use such a term, lies outside the biblical text. It lies in patterns of response to God which marked the first people in Israel to move towards monotheism, and which were renewed and perfected in the lifestyle, the teaching and the commitments of Jesus and his first followers. We would know nothing of these patterns without Scripture, but they do not in any sense depend on Scripture for their validity. They are, perhaps we might say, the canon *outside* the canon – not unlike Irenaeus' 'canon of truth'.

Thus 'biblical monotheism' is a very adequate *shorthand* for the expression of such patterns of thought and conduct in Israel before Jesus, and 'New Testament faith' for the fresh stage represented by Jesus and by those who came to believe through his life, death and resurrection. But if we press these expressions in order to tie them to precisely these books of the Bible, or to suggest that the patterns of religious response involved can be found only in Scripture and equally distributed throughout

Scripture, we shall falsify what Theissen is saying, making Christians a 'people of the book' in an unacceptable sense.

Central to Theissen's thesis is the conviction that the Christian faith as he presents it is not simply one way of understanding God and the world which is sanctioned by the Bible, and which Lutherans are likely to prefer, while Calvinists or Catholics or Anglicans may prefer others among the pluralism of voices to be heard within Scripture. On the contrary, what he calls for short 'biblical faith' is the faith for which Jesus of Nazareth lived and died – not in the text but in history – and to which modern people are challenged by God to commit themselves. If you like, it is what Theissen understands to be 'the gospel'. It existed before the Gospels and would continue to exist even if the Gospels perished. As Irenaeus put it, 'Even if the apostles had not left us any writings, would it not be necessary to follow the course of the tradition which they handed down to those to whom they committed the churches?'[6] Of course 'tradition' here does not mean ecclesiastical tradition *as against* Scripture; it means 'the gospel', the basic faith that existed before there was a Scripture. The same may be said of the Reformation appeal to Scripture against tradition, which is an appeal to Scripture as enshrining this primitive gospel – not Scripture as a self-contained text which would be binding independently of the faith it taught. The Bible speaks, falteringly and unevenly, but enough for us to grasp it, of this faith; but it is the faith, not the Bible, that we believe in.

II

One may ask, of course: 'How do we know that we ought to be committed to such a pattern of belief and action? How do we know that the development of biblical monotheism was a good thing, or that Jesus of Nazareth was a good thing?' Whatever the answer to this question, it cannot be, 'Because the Bible says so'. The Bible, taken as a whole in all its amorphous variety, does not exactly say so; and even if it did, that would still not compel us to believe it. What this discussion makes clear is that the exposition of the Bible cannot in itself produce theological truth: the resolution of truth-questions raised by the Bible cannot be settled by appeal to the Bible.

There is thus an important sense in which biblical scholars as such are not and cannot be theologians, for a theologian is one concerned directly with theological truth; though of course they may *also* be theologians, as Theissen is. This would seem almost too obvious to need saying, were it not that many theologians do seem to think that biblical exposition is in itself a way of deciding questions of truth in the real world. Of course it is probably not possible to decide whether the gospel is true on *any* purely objective grounds. No one can be coerced into seeing Jesus of Nazareth as a genuine advance in the development of human religion and indeed of the human race. If you really cannot see a cause for rejoicing in the faithfulness to death and subsequent vindication of the one John Robinson called 'the Man for others'[7] – rather than in the aggressive self-promotion and survival of the fittest 'man for himself' – you cannot be argued into it. Our case is not that the gospel *can* be proved by arguments that belong outside the realm of biblical study, but simply that it certainly *cannot* be proved by arguments internal to the world of biblical study. In advancing theological claims we are making statements about the way things really are and really have come about – metaphysical and historical claims; and these cannot be roped off from the enquiries of philosophers and historians by saying that they are 'biblical' truths. What Theissen has so signally achieved is to break out of the closed circle by advancing propositions about the essence of the Christian gospel on the basis of historical study of the Bible, which must then take their chance in the public arena alongside other accounts of the nature of reality and of human history and evolution.

Our account of the relation of faith to the Bible has a clear bearing on the old question of 'revelation', which was touched on in the last chapter. Since what is believed is relatively independent of the Bible, despite the fact that the Bible is a primary witness to it, it is difficult (if not impossible) to speak of the Christian faith as 'revealed' through Scripture. It is this faith that causes there to be anything to be put in writing and canonized as Scripture, not the other way around. One way to express this is perhaps to say that the Bible is not revelation about an unknown God, but a document that witnesses to the relationship of people with a God who is already known before Scripture is written.[8] It may be that for us some truths about God could not be known if they were not in Scripture – though it is notoriously difficult to say which truths these are – but this is true, if it is true, only *per accidens*. The fact that they are written down has perhaps prevented them from being lost, but in principle they were known before they were written down. In fact I am uneasy about this whole way of thinking, and should much prefer to say that God's input into the human situation involves events and human responses to these events, as well as ideas and concepts that can be recorded in writing. 'Revelation', if that is the right word to use, operates throughout the whole historical process by which people have had dealings with God from the beginning, not just in and through their relationship to a sacred text. And as Maurice Wiles showed in his Bampton Lectures,[9] to untangle the relation of divine and human causality here is a task of the utmost intricacy – certainly not one for a biblical specialist to attempt.

The central question, in any case, is not whether there has been revelation as opposed to a putative 'natural' knowledge of God, and if so, where it is to be located. The central question is whether or not human beings really have come to know God and can still do so. The existence and contents of both Old and New Testaments witness, as the Open University syllabus used to put it, to 'Man's Religious Quest'; the question for faith is whether it was the true God to whom this quest was directed, and if so, whether it succeeded. Faith affirms that indeed it did – of course only through God's own desire to become known; but it succeeded before a record of it was written down. Indeed, what is written in the Bible, with rare exceptions such as certain prophetic oracles, is presented as human words about God, not as words of God to man. We made this point in the last chapter by speaking of 'wisdom' literature rather than prophecy as the norm, for the Old Testament at least. The Bible is people's reflection on their relationship with the known God: the knowledge, or revelation if you like, lies behind it rather than in it.

III

Some of what we have been saying about the gradual development of a true knowledge of God in Israel and in primitive Christianity – a development which we can learn about through the Bible but which is not identical with the Bible – may sound uncomfortably like the old idea of progressive revelation. Has not twentieth-century biblical study abandoned this old notion, never to return to it?[10] Certainly there does seem to be a cherub with a flaming sword posted at the entrance to that particular bit of the liberals' paradise. The theory of progressive revelation failed for many reasons. It was too simplistic; it was too tied to now untenable versions of the theory of evolution, perhaps even to versions concocted by theologians and historians and never actually held by scientists; it was too optimistic about human capacity for progress to stand much chance of seeming plausible to the heirs of two World Wars; it was even perhaps latently anti-semitic in relativizing the Old Testament as mere preparation for Christ. In its classic form I would not wish to defend it. Yet it was a serious attempt to do justice to two facts to which more recent theories of biblical theology do not always give full and equal weight. On the one hand, God was really known in Israel before

Jesus, and indeed before there was any written record of this knowledge; and on the other hand, some of what was believed about him cannot have been true, if what is known through Jesus *is* true.

The image of *progress* was of course thoroughly misleading, for some of the most essential insights arrived early on the scene: indeed, if Julius Wellhausen was right, some of them were lost to view as time went on, so that the development of faith had elements of decline as well as of progress.[11] But the idea that knowledge of the true God has a history, to which the Bible gives us access but of which it is not as it stands a fully accurate record, so that we must in some measure get behind it rather than studying the text in its present, smooth form – this idea seems to me inherent in the Christian faith. We have, through God's own grace, acquired a knowledge of him, and salient points in our acquiring it can in principle be named: it does not come about through the existence of a sacred text, but through the living of the life of the people of God, which continues down to the present. This approach, like that of progressive revelation, is not primarily a theory about Scripture, and like progressive revelation it would fail if it were. It is a historical claim about how the human race actually came by the knowledge of God which Christians claim to have, a claim which appeals to Scripture primarily as part of its supporting evidence.

IV

When all this is said, however, we still have not finished with the role and authority of the Bible. I have spoken, in a very Anglo-Saxon way, of events and ideas to which the Bible gives us access, and of *knowledge* as the aim of our biblical study. The Bible thus appears as a source book for correct theology, for thinking the right thoughts about God. All this I would defend, but would want to add something from the German tradition in which Theissen stands. It is this: what our study of the Bible ultimately presents us with is not a body of knowledge or a corpus of doctrine which we have to assimilate, but a divine challenge to which we have to respond. Indeed, one may make the point by drawing a contrast that is, strangely enough, much easier in English than it is in German, and say that what we learn from our study of Scripture is not biblical *belief* but precisely biblical *faith*. The biblical text mediates not information or opinion but encounter.

We thus return here to a point made in the first chapter: Christians are nourished in their faith by reading the Bible, not simply by contemplating truths they have extracted from it. If the first part of our reconstruction of a model for biblical authority today concentrated on the Bible as historical evidence, and the second on the Bible as a source of theological insight into the faith for which Jesus lived and died, a third remains to be explored. This is the way in which reading these texts can be a channel whereby the God of the Bible is still encountered in the present, to call forth faith and to enkindle hope. And that means that the question of biblical hermeneutics must be given a proper consideration. The decision to leave this question till late in the book has been a deliberate one, for I think that it has played far too important a role in modern discussion of the Bible, deflecting attention from many of the other issues we have been considering; also I do not think it the primary question about the Bible, for the very reasons discussed in this chapter. For I believe that Christians exist principally in relation not to a text but to a person. But that is not to say that the hermeneutical question is an empty one, and we shall turn to it next.

Notes

1. J. Barr, 'Childs' Introduction to the Old Testament as Scripture', *Journal for the Study of the Old Testament* 16 (1980), pp. 12–23; quotation from p. 21.

2. D. H. Kelsey, *The Uses of Scripture in Recent Theology*, Philadelphia and London 1975.

3. G. Theissen, *Biblical Faith: an Evolutionary Approach*, London 1984.

4. The last two lines of Tennyson's 'In Memoriam'. For the theories of Teilhard, see P. Teilhard de Chardin, *The Phenomenon of Man*, London 1960; *The Future of Man*, London 1964; *The Appearance of Man*, London 1965; and *Christianity and Evolution*, London 1971.

5. R. Dawkins, *The Selfish Gene*, New York and Oxford 1976.

6. Irenaeus, *adversus haereses* iii.4.1.

7. See J. A. T. Robinson, *Honest to God* (London 1963), pp. 64–83.

8. I owe this formulation to James Barr: see esp. his *Old and New in Interpretation* (London 1966), pp. 89–92; also *The Bible in the Modern World* (London 1973), pp. 115–16 and *Holy Scripture: Canon, Authority, Criticism* (Philadelphia and Oxford 1983), pp. 1–6.

9. M. F. Wiles, *God's Action in the World*, London 1986.

10. See the penetrating criticism in J. W. Rogerson, 'Progressive Revelation: its History and Value as a Key to Old Testament Interpretation', *Epworth Review* 9 (1982), pp. 73–86. C. H. Dodd's *The Authority of the Bible*, London 1929, was perhaps the last and most persuasive attempt to give an account of scriptural authority on the basis of a theory of progressive revelation.

11. See J. Wellhausen, *Prolegomena to the History of Israel*, Edinburgh 1885; repr. as *Prolegomena to the History of Ancient Israel*, New York 1957.

CHAPTER 6

Salvation by Hermeneutics

'The wisdom of God in a mystery'

I have stressed what I have been calling the 'logical space' between the Christian faith and the Christian Bible so strongly because my perception of the current trend in Christian thinking is that we have moved into a somewhat biblicist phase, where anything less than an equation of biblical ways of thought with the faith itself is seen as a 'liberal' watering-down of religion to what 'modern man' can swallow. On the contrary, I have argued, Christianity cannot survive if it is simply reduced to the Bible. Indeed, the Bible itself is the first thing to suffer in such an arrangement, by being made to bear a burden it is ill-equipped to sustain. Only if it is recognized that authority does not lie only with the Bible can the Bible achieve the authority that does properly belong to it.

Nevertheless, the truth that the faith preceded the Bible, could in principle survive without it, and is not exhausted by what is in the Bible, must not lead us to exaggerate: Christianity still is in some recognizable sense the religion of a book. Christianity and Judaism have not been content to remain orally transmitted faiths. Both have decided that a particular set of texts is to serve as the record of their origins and nature, and are content to see these texts used as the vehicle by which they explain and commend themselves to outsiders, and by which insiders are nurtured and sustained in their faith. So far I have necessarily concentrated on how essential it is to see the Bible as a text which we can get behind, for people have been telling us now for fifty years at least that this is just what we cannot and must not do, and there is no sign that they are going to stop. Indeed, movements like canonical criticism and narrative theology seem determined that digging up the text is to be made absolutely illicit in all circumstances. In this context I have thought it right to mount a defence, not just of the permissibility, but of the necessity of such excavative work. It remains true, however, that we still have the text, and we are charged by our faith not only to study it and to use it as a means of getting in touch with our roots, but to read it as spiritual nourishment as it is; and it is this that must concern us now.

I

The Bible, we said in the last chapter, is not the revelation of an unknown God, but human reflection on the God who is posited as already well known, and on the means by which he has become known.[1] Primary revelation lies before and outside the text of Scripture. Nevertheless, the knowledge of God to which the Bible is a witness is mediated not only through life in the Christian community, but also through an encounter with Scripture itself. Indeed, part of belonging to the Christian community is a continual reading of Scripture, especially in worship. And Christian experience bears out the power of these particular texts to illuminate the minds and hearts of succeeding generations.[2]

It is true that to *some* extent this can be seen as an effect rather than a cause of their scriptural status. As structuralists (among others) have stressed, qualities like 'profundity' lie in some measure in the eye of the beholder.[3] The designation of a couple of sentences as a 'poem' can make us find in it all kinds of qualities of closure, complexity and subtlety that we should not find if we were told that the same lines were random scribblings. In the same way the announcement that a work is a religious classic – or still more *the* religious classic – predisposes us to see depths in it that we might otherwise fail to perceive. But this is true, in my judgement, only at the margins of the canon. Canonizing the Song of Songs has indeed led people to find in it religious teachings, and also a degree of moral seriousness, that no one would dream of ascribing to it if it turned up out of a biblical context in a jar near the Dead Sea. And I doubt if we should see *much* worth preserving in Nahum or 3 John if they were not officially Scripture. But there are few books now in the Bible we should think unimportant or trivial, wherever we encountered them. Most of them have what Leslie Houlden calls 'theological class';[4] they would belong to the classics of religious literature even if they had never been canonized – though whether they would have survived to become so is of course another question. The 'authority' of Scripture in the sense of its religious and literary excellence and its inherent, not merely attributed, power to inform the minds of those who read it seems to me beyond argument.

There was a time when an emphasis on the literary qualities of the Bible was deeply suspect in theological circles, as smacking of a certain lack of religious seriousness. *The Bible, Designed to be Read as Literature,*[5] one of the earliest attempts to arrange biblical books thematically and to print them like a modern text, rather than in double columns, found no great acclaim in the theological world. Theologians and churchmen no doubt felt it should have been called *The Bible, Designed to Lie on Coffee-Tables*. As Austin Farrer remarked, there is poetry in the Bible in which 'the unreclaimed humanist in us' may feel 'he is getting his familiar food; but we must also have a faint awareness that we are being allowed a holiday from the proper business of the Old Testament Muse'[6] – which is to convey the word of *God*.

But 'the Bible as literature' is now a booming concern, especially in America, and the idea that the Bible should be treated as a literary classic is well established. Among many examples, we may think of Northrop Frye's *The Great Code*,[7] or Frank Kermode's study of the Gospel according to St Mark, *The Genesis of Secrecy*,[8] or indeed of the recent *Literary Guide to the Bible*.[9] In this sense 'the text itself', rather than what lies behind or before or outside the text, is important for both theology and literary studies in a way that it has not been for a long time: certainly more important than it has been since the rise of critical biblical scholarship and perhaps (if my suggestions about the way the Bible actually functioned in earlier times are correct) for much longer than that. Perhaps, indeed, the text 'in itself' has *never* been so important before. As we have seen, generations of Christians for whom the Bible, the whole Bible, and nothing but the Bible, was entirely authoritative nevertheless did not read it with such an eye for unity and wholeness as modern literary readers, or as those who have made canonicity into an interpretative as well as a formal principle. For many modern Christians as for many modern literary critics the interpretation of the Bible as a 'work', a single literary and religious classic text, has moved to the centre of interest.

One very salutary effect of this fresh enthusiasm for the Bible as a text, despite the difficulties already hinted at, is that it sets a high premium on what used to be called the perspicuity of Scripture. Interpretation is not the derivation from Scripture of arcane secrets; it does not depend on detecting difficulties in the text which hint, for the initiated, at dark mysteries lying beneath the surface; it does not treat the Bible as essentially oracular in character. The relevance and freshness of the Bible, which gives it its character as a 'classic', is not a matter of being timeless in the sense of free-floating, a collection of mysterious words awaiting an interpreter to achieve meaning. As with any other classic, its relevance is a function of its power to communicate truth even across the cultural divide separating us from its first authors.

The 'authority' of a classic in this sense is quite different from the authority of a holy text whose meaning can be determined only by those in the know. Sacred texts, as we have seen, tend to be semantically indeterminate, for they have to be read as supporting the religious system to which they belong, even at the expense of their natural sense. There is no doubt that the attribution of authority to the Christian Bible has frequently resulted in just the same thing happening there. But to call the Bible a 'classic' is not to make it authoritative – and hence semantically vacuous – in that way. It is to say that it has within itself the power to illuminate ever-new situations, even beyond the confines of its original cultural context.

II

The act of interpretation by which we come to understand such works as belonging both supremely to their own time and yet, paradoxically, to our own age and potentially to every age, may be called the hermeneutical act. To my mind few modern writers have analysed it more acutely than George Steiner, in his *After Babel*.[10] Though what he says there is said primarily of the particular hermeneutical process that is involved in translation, his remarks are applicable generally to understanding texts from other cultures – or indeed from other minds than our own, which means, therefore, all texts. Interpretation is not a subtype of translation, as in the notorious 'translation model' of reading the Bible;[11] rather, translation is a subtype of interpretation. But the advantage of considering hermeneutical questions through translation theory, as Steiner does, is that we can more easily disentangle different elements in interpretation where the need to pass from one language to another makes them stand out.

Steiner identifies four stages in the interpretative act, or what he calls (following Schleiermacher) the 'hermeneutic motion'.[12] The first stage is the act of trust towards the text: the charitable assumption that there is something there worth understanding. At times, of course, this may be a mistake. With some texts we may find, as Dorothy Parker put it, that there is considerably less here than meets the eye. But if an initial reading provides a *prima facie* justification for going further, there follows a second stage, in which we make as it were a raid on the text, invading it with our own questions and trying to get, as we often say, 'inside' it. Then, thirdly, we bring it home and naturalize it within our own system of thinking – make it part, if you like, of our own private literary canon, allow it to speak to our own concerns and to stand alongside the products of our own mind. The second stage corresponds perhaps roughly to the *subtilitas intelligendi* of traditional hermeneutics, the procedure by which the sense of the text is grasped, the third to the *subtilitas explicandi*, in which we play its ideas back to ourselves in our own language, so that our understanding is no longer mute.[13] Both stages are plainly involved in all exegesis.

But there is for Steiner a fourth stage, and it is this which is peculiarly important in identifying a work as a classic. At the fourth stage an equilibrium is reached between the world of the text and the world of the reader. A good translation, says Steiner – and we may add, a good interpretation – includes, beyond the acts of appropriation and naturalization, an act of restitution, a renewed distancing of the text, as it were giving it back to its author while yet retaining it for oneself. 'What the author wrote' and 'what I have made of him' thereby achieve equipoise. A real meeting of minds has occurred across what may be a great cultural divide, and there is something new in the world: an old text which yet exists, unclouded by misunderstanding, within the modern context.[14] Only great works enable us to achieve this fully, transcending cultural gaps yet without losing their own cultural context. A definition of a classic might lie along this road. As compared with more ephemeral works, it neither resists incorporation in an alien culture, becoming simply trivial when detached from its original setting, nor adapts so readily as to be in effect merely a *tabula rasa* on which new meanings can be inscribed at will. It remains itself, yet has something fresh to say to each new enquirer.

It seems to me that biblical hermeneutics, the act of interpreting the Bible, aims at achieving this fourth stage in relation to the biblical text. This is part of its trust that the Bible above all texts is capable of such richness and classicality. Conversely, the fact that the modern reader can and does so often succeed in arriving at this stage in reading the Bible is a kind of empirical confirmation that the Bible is indeed a classic, and has the kind of authority that Christians attribute to it. In both Judaism and Christianity, the power of the biblical word to become present to the attentive reader has always been a central way in which God has been encountered. Thus, by teasing out the way the reading of biblical texts proceeds, along the lines indicated by Steiner, we have found a way of describing the unique authority of the Bible from the point of view of hermeneutical theory. The trend towards 'literary' readings of Scripture will strongly confirm that the Bible is indeed in the required sense a classic text, able to speak a living word in the present from its anchorage in the past.

III

Now this account of hermeneutics may be surprising, for it hardly accords with the way the term is used in much modern theology. One way of putting the difference is to say that traditionally in aesthetic theory (as here for Steiner) 'hermeneutics' means an account of how understanding works; whereas in biblical studies it tends to be used as a name for attempts to solve the perceived problem that understanding does *not* work. Theologians talk about a hermeneutical gap between the modern reader and the biblical text, which they need to find some way of bridging – a cultural divide which means that the text no longer 'speaks', so that some technique has to be devised to give it a voice once more.

Another way of putting it is to say that hermeneutics is traditionally the name of a *discipline*, the study of how meaning is perceived and interpreted, whereas in theology it is more often the title of a *programme*, *'a* hermeneutic' – that is, a code of techniques which will accomplish the task of making it possible for the modern Christian to appropriate the Bible. The point is made with absolute clarity though in horrible jargon by G. Ebeling: 'Interpretation, and therefore hermeneutics, is required only in cases where the "word-event" is for some reason disturbed.'[15] The 'New Hermeneutic', with which Ebeling is associated, was accordingly not a new theory about how meaning occurs in texts and how we come to understand such meaning: it was a proposal about the kinds of meanings we *ought to* perceive in the biblical text if it was to continue to be relevant to us.

These differences of perception are extremely important. Central to them, I believe, is the loss of the sense that Scripture is perspicuous. Many newer hermeneutical proposals in practice seem to unite modern interpreters with early Christians like Origen, struggling with a Bible that did not say quite what they wanted it to say. Both groups are divided from the men of the Renaissance and the Reformation who wanted to insist that the Bible spoke plain words that all could understand. Incidentally, they are also divided from Schleiermacher, the father of modern hermeneutics, whose great breakthrough lay precisely in his discovery that questions of interpretation are most interesting where we do understand, rather than, as for the great allegorizers, where we do not.[16] And they are also thereby divided from those today who have suddenly rediscovered the Bible as a translucent literary corpus with power to free and fire the imagination. This is worth saying, because I do not believe this division is always perceived. Many biblical conservatives feel the 'Bible as literature' movement to be their ally. In this, however, I am sure they are mistaken.

What unites both pre- and post-critical hermeneutical *programmes* is what, in the light of our earlier discussions, we may see as an attempt to find too much meaning in the biblical text. This results from a clash between the extreme authority which is attributed to it and the apparently problematic character, for the believing community, of its plain sense. Early Christian exegetes, of whom Origen may serve as the type, saw the authority of the whole Bible as implying in effect that it was a Christian book through and through. For them, as we noted in chapter 2, the sense that the Old Testament was a Jewish book with meanings that did not belong in the Christian dispensation was quickly lost. It was therefore imperative that it should be so interpreted that it could have a determining influence on Christian life and thought. At the same time, the Church's developing rule of faith made it perfectly plain that some of the surface meanings of the scriptural text could not possibly be accepted as binding. Consequently Scripture became a problem, whose solution could only lie through the development of 'a hermeneutic' in the strong, prog-rammatic sense: a set of devices that would extract edifying meanings from an unedifying text.

Now my impression is that the motive force behind much of the modern interest in hermeneutics in theology is not so very different. Hermeneutics in this sense seems to interest primarily people who combine a high view of scriptural authority with a critical awareness of the cultural gap separating us from the Bible. They thus belong to the whole movement of thought in modern theology which asks how the Bible can still be heard as authorita-tive and inspiring Scripture 'after all': how we can accept critical approaches *and yet still* hear the Bible as the Word of God; how we can reclaim the Scriptures for faith and for theology *despite* what the critics have done. I suspect that there is sometimes bad faith here. Sophisticated hermeneutical moves can enable conserva-tive biblicists to continue in their biblicism by circumventing the problems raised by critical study.[17]

But this is not the whole story. Some impeccably critical scholars share the biblicist perception of critical study as essen-tially something that has cut us off from the Bible – distanced it from us. Hence, they argue, even if we fully accept the validity of biblical criticism, we need to move on from it, so that the Bible can once again (though now doubtless post-critically rather than pre-critically) become 'Scripture' for us, rather than just a collection of dated old texts. Something like this perception undoubtedly lies at the root of 'canonical criticism', exactly as it did at the root of the 'biblical theology' movement for which canonical criticism is intended as a replacement.[18] Against this whole style of thinking, I should want to say that the gap between ourselves and the text is exaggerated in the first place: not, indeed, that there is no gap, but that the gap becomes a *problem* only if we start with an exaggerated view of biblical authority. Of course if we expect the Bible to be simply a modern book, answering all our present questions in black and white, as fundamentalists do, or as many Christians of Origen's day did, then we shall find critical study immensely disturbing. But the difficulty is largely of our own making, because we have set up a false alternative: either the Bible is immediately contemporary with us, or it is mere antiquarian nonsense. This is the thin end of the wedge[19] in a new guise. In fact we do not experience this kind of polarization with other great texts from the past. No one ever supposes that because Shakespeare is not modern, he is therefore unable to speak to us at all.

Now my suggestion is that the modern literary perception of the Bible as a classic, for all that it has been seized on gleefully by some hermeneutically inclined conservatives, can in fact help to break this most unhelpful mould. The literary understanding of biblical authority as the inherent authority of a classic work arises not from sophisticated hermeneutical techniques, but from attention to the plain sense of the text, which is rightly felt to have the power and scope that only great works of literature possess.[20] The hermeneutical question is then not a question of how we can make something useful out of antique rubbish, but how we can best appropriate – and critically evaluate – literature that already speaks powerfully to us. Hermeneutics is thus not the solution of a difficulty, but the contemplation of a mystery.[21]

It is, let me repeat, not critical study of the Bible that produces a problem in relating it to modern questions. Critical study as such never tries to force this issue to the fore anyway, but is content to let the text illuminate the modern world where it may. It is biblicistic claims about the authority of the Bible – or even traditional Protestant claims about it – that generate a climate in which any historical grounding of the text at once raises 'problems' about its relevance to us. If critical scholars have rarely been attracted by complex hermeneutical programmes, this has not usually been because they have been obsessed with 'merely' historical features of the text and therefore uninterested in appropriating the Bible today. It is because their awareness of its relevance and their sense of its power has been a matter of course, the motive that led them to study it in the first place. Hermeneutical programmes tend to appeal to those who would never read the Bible if they did not think it was infallible, and who therefore need some way of retaining its infallibility when all the obvious supports of it have been shot away. For those who never thought it infallible in the first place, complicated shoring-up operations are largely superfluous.

We may go even further, and say that hermeneutical problems have moved to the centre of concern in modern theology partly through a certain failure of nerve in modern religious faith, producing a nervous desire for the Bible to provide the answers that we cannot find for ourselves. This is a long way from the confidence of, for example, the Reformers that there was nothing to fear from a free and open reading of the Bible, because it spoke of the same faith that they themselves already had. Some words of Gerd Theissen seem to me to capture this very tellingly, and in the process to point to the right way to see hermeneutical questions in relation to the Bible today:

> Here, to my mind, is the heart of the problem of interpretation. The Bible comes alive where authentic religious experience coincides with texts which are themselves testimony to an authentic religious experience: the past strikes a spark off the present or the present off the past, and both are illuminated. The chief reason why religious texts from the past are so difficult to understand is that modern man has become uncertain of his own religious experience. He mistrusts it, and expects his encounter with the past to supply information which he will obtain only if he is truly concerned with religious questions and experiences . . . Only one conclusion can be drawn from the problem as we have described it: it is important to be aware of one's present religious experiences and to articulate the degree of independence which they have from the past . . . so that it then becomes possible to enter into a dialogue with the past which is no longer expected to meet the impossible demand that the present should be legitimated by the past. Such a dialogue would be open to the past. And again and again we shall have the pleasant surprise of finding unexpected allies there, indeed a better way of expressing things, which can give a new stimulus to religious life in the present.[22]

IV

In this chapter I have been arguing in many ways *ad hominem*. The hermeneutical tradition in modern theology, with its increasing valuation of the finished form of the text as a literary entity which communicates with the modern reader directly, is finding favour with biblical conservatives as a way of avoiding the challenges of biblical criticism. 'The Bible as literature' used to be the refuge of the sceptic, a way of retaining the literary value of the Bible while avoiding its religious claims. Now it has become the ally of the biblicists, who can use it to circumvent the doubts and difficulties which honest historical enquiry into the Bible raises by claiming that a historical reading of the Bible is deeply philistine, and would never be tolerated in secular literary studies. It will be abundantly clear by now that I do not in the least share the conservative distaste for critical historical enquiry into the Bible, and think the whole attack misconceived. Nevertheless, the striking insights that literary studies have given us into biblical texts should not be discarded, just because fundamentalism likes them too.

A deeper appreciation of how literary interpretation and understanding work does indeed support the claim that the Bible works on us as a literary classic *in addition to* (not in place of) the other functions it has in the Christian faith. We may not only grant this to the enthusiasts for hermeneutics for the sake of argument; we should accept it with open arms. For what follows from it is not at all that the Bible is therefore encased in a protective covering of literary excellence that gives it a kind of diplomatic immunity from historical investigation. What follows is that the Bible is one of those supreme texts whose continuing classic status goes hand in hand with its essential rootedness in its own age. The Bible is not a *tabula rasa* on which each age can write its own agenda. On the contrary, in Northrop Frye's words, 'this huge, sprawling, tactless book sit[s] there inscrutably in the middle of our cultural heritage, frustrating all our efforts to walk around it'.[23] The Bible as literature only superficially seems to lead away from historical criticism and into the safe haven of biblicism, where no sharp breezes of scepticism can blow. Once we really begin to see what is involved in understanding such a work, we find ourselves washed back out into the sea of history and of particularity.

Notes

1. See above, p. 55.

2. cf. my article, 'The Place of the Bible in Moral Debate', *Theology* 88 (1985), pp. 204–9.

3. cf. my *Reading the Old Testament: Method in Biblical Study* (Philadelphia and London 1984), pp. 228–9.

4. See J. L. Houlden's review of P. Curtis, *A Hawk among Sparrows: A Biography of Austin Farrer*, in *Theology* 89 (1986), p. 67.

5. E. S. Bates, ed. and arr., *The Bible, Designed to be Read as Literature*, London 1937.

6. A. M. Farrer, *The Glass of Vision* (London 1948), p. 124.

7. Northrop Frye, *The Great Code: The Bible and Literature*, London, Melbourne and Henley 1982.

8. F. Kermode, *The Genesis of Secrecy: on the Interpretation of Narrative*, Cambridge, Mass., and London 1979.

9. R. Alter and F. Kermode, ed., *The Literary Guide to the Bible*, London 1987.

10. G. Steiner, *After Babel: Aspects of Language and Translation*, New York and London 1975.

11. The idea that the business of theology is to 'translate' the Bible into modern terms has been pervasive in Christian theological hermeneutics, and the image was perhaps specially influential in the so-called 'New Hermeneutic' associated with G. Ebeling and E. Fuchs: see G. Ebeling, *Word and Faith*, London 1963, and E. Fuchs, *Zum hermeneutischen Problem in der Theologie*, Tübingen 1960. The standard introduction to the New Hermeneutic is J. M. Robinson and J. B. Cobb, eds, *New Frontiers in Theology: II, The New Hermeneutic*, New York 1964. Cf. also A. C. Thiselton, *The Two Horizons: New Testament Hermeneutics and Philosophical Description with Special Reference to Heidegger, Bultmann, Gadamer, and Wittgenstein*, Exeter 1980. For a criticism of the 'translation' model, see D. H. Kelsey, *The Uses of Scripture in Recent Theology* (Philadelphia 1975), pp. 185–210 and James Barr's review of Kelsey in *The Virginia Seminary Journal* 30–1 (1978–9), pp. 39–40.

12. Steiner, *After Babel*, pp. 296–413.

13. The distinction goes back to J. Ernesti, *Institutio Interpretis Novi Testamenti* (Leipzig 1761), chapter 1, § 4. Schleiermacher's discussion denies that the *subtilitas explicandi* is properly part of hermeneutics – see *Hermeneutics: the Handwritten Manuscripts by Friedrich Schleiermacher*, ed. H. Kimmerle (Missoula, Mont., 1977), p. 41.

14. Steiner, *After Babel*, pp. 300–2.

15. G. Ebeling, 'Wort Gottes und Hermeneutik', *Zeitschrift für Theologie und Kirche* 56 (1959), pp. 224–51; my translation.

16. Schleiermacher certainly saw hermeneutics as active rather than passive, a 'motion' of the interpreter towards the text rather than a passive receiving of signals from it. But it is a distortion of this insight to argue that the role of the interpreter is a *creative* one in the sense that it means forcing the text to answer our questions rather than attending to the questions it was written to answer. Indeed, Schleiermacher's insistence that the *subtilitas explicandi* is not properly part of hermeneutics (see note 13) seems designed to prevent this misunderstanding.

17. cf. the wise words of Krister Stendahl: 'I wonder if some of our attempts at literary analysis – be it structuralism or not so new "new criticism" – are not, when all is said and done, a form of apologetics, sophisticated to a degree which obfuscates the apologetic intention even to its practitioners' ('The Bible as a Classic and the Bible as Holy Scripture', *Journal of Biblical Literature* 103 (1984), pp. 3–10; quotation from p. 6).

18. cf. B. S. Childs, *Biblical Theology in Crisis*, Philadelphia 1970, and the comments of J. Barr, *Holy Scripture: Canon, Authority, Criticism* (Philadelphia and Oxford 1983), pp. 142–6.

19. cf. above, p. 12.

20. cf. again Stendahl's remarks quoted in note 17 above.

21. On this see my two-part article 'Reflections on Cultural Relativism', *Theology* 82 (1979), pp. 103–9 and 191–9, with reference to Steiner.

22. G. Theissen, *On Having a Critical Faith* (London 1979), p. 82.

23. Frye, *The Great Code*, pp. xviii–xix.

CHAPTER 7

The Bible in Liturgy

'This is the Word of the Lord'

Until the first major revision of its daily lectionary in 1871 the Church of England read the Bible in whole chapters, troubling little about the appropriateness of the chapter divisions in the English Bible. One little-known effect of this was that on three occasions in the year the second lesson at Evensong ended as follows: 'Paul . . . beckoned with the hand unto the people. And when there was made a great silence, he spake unto them in the Hebrew tongue, saying, Here endeth the second lesson' (Acts 21.40 AV). But not all liturgical change is for the better; and on Quinquagesima Sunday we may now hear the story of a man caught gathering sticks on the sabbath, which concludes with the memorable words: 'And the Lord said to Moses, "The man shall be put to death; all the congregation shall stone him with stones outside the camp." And all the congregation brought him outside the camp, and stoned him to death with stones, as the Lord commanded Moses: this is the Word of the Lord' (Num. 15.35–36).

The case for what we have called a logical space between the Bible and the Christian faith is thrown into sharp relief by the effect the formula 'This is the Word of the Lord' has on a congregation which has been following the lessons with reasonable attention. Sometimes it will provoke an angry reaction. I have certainly heard angry snorts and grunts when the formula has concluded either Old Testament passages about the retributive judgement of God or New Testament rulings about the subordinate place of women in the Church. Not infrequently the indignation is then generalized into a root-and-branch opposition to reading the Bible in church, as if it were largely or even entirely composed of such material. Stepping back a little from that brink, people then sometimes argue for a much more highly selective reading, and propose what must amount to a canon within the canon. Lectionaries do of course in practice operate with a reduced canon: it is simply that there is not a complete consensus on how restricted it should be, and a system such as that of the Church of England inevitably leaves in some passages many would prefer to see excised. It is far from my purpose to argue against this selectivity in the liturgical reading of Scripture. I am not one of those who would like to bring back the cursing psalms, or make the book of Judges the staple diet for Sunday mornings. But though selection is a good practical solution to the difficulty, it does not engage with the serious underlying problem. The amount of material in the Bible which is unedifying to an offensive extent is not great, and one can very easily select enough lessons for one, two, or three years without making any conscious decisions to avoid it: so much of the Bible cries out to be read, there is not space for it all in a Sunday lectionary anyway. But seen from another vantage-point the unedifying material points to a much larger and more genuine problem about the formula 'This is the Word of the Lord'.

We can begin to sense this problem by noticing that much of the Bible that is read liturgically, while inoffensive, is not religiously inspiring either. We jib at 'Samuel hewed Agag in pieces before the Lord in Gilgal: this is the Word of the Lord' (1 Sam. 15.33); but what about 'So they cast off the anchors and left them in the sea, at the same time loosening the ropes that tied the rudders; then hoisting the foresail to the wind they made for the beach: this is the Word of the Lord' (Acts 27.40)? 'Word of God' language strongly suggests, of course, the prophetic paradigm (cf. 2 Pet. 1.19–21), or perhaps the paradigm of God giving the law through Moses. We expect that God will speak through this passage. The problem is not so much the (rather rare) occasions when the 'word' he is heard uttering is morally objectionable, as the far more numerous occasions when the words of the text are not naturally read according to this prophetic model at all. To return to a way of speaking that proved useful in previous chapters, much of the Bible is manifestly not prophetic in this sense: it is human reflection or 'wisdom', narrative, hymnody, advice, anything but divine oracles.[1]

I

What the liturgical error of forcing the prophetic paradigm on us has usefully done, in fact, is to draw our attention to the diversity of genres within the Bible, and to require us to give some account of this within any theory of scriptural authority. In recent years it is perhaps Paul Ricoeur who, particularly in his essay 'Toward a Hermeneutic of the Idea of Revelation',[2] has taken most seriously the need to make theological sense of the fact that Scripture contains genres which cannot be assimilated to the model of divine communication to men.

Ricoeur points out that the diversity of genres in the Bible is irreducible. When the Nicene Creed declares Christian faith in the Holy Spirit 'who spoke by the prophets', it encourages us to assimilate all of Scripture to the prophetic paradigm. This

> leads to the idea of scripture as dictated, as something whispered in someone's ear. The idea of revelation is then confused with the idea of a double author of sacred texts, and any access to a less subjective manner of understanding revelation is prematurely cut off . . . The . . . idea of inspiration . . . is deprived of the enrichment it might receive from those forms of discourse which are less easily interpreted in terms of a voice behind a voice or of a double author of scripture.[3]

On the contrary, Ricoeur argues, we ought to give a positive account of the fact that the Bible presents us with revelation not as direct divine speech but embodied in narrative, law, wisdom, hymns, prayers, and thanksgivings. 'The literary genres of the Bible do not constitute a rhetorical facade which it would be possible to pull down in order to reveal some thought content that is indifferent to its literary vehicle.'[4] If indeed revelation is the right word to use for what is mediated to us through the Bible, then we shall have to understand revelation far less as the direct communication of information by God, and far more as the fruit of an encounter into which the biblical text leads us. This it does by involving us in a story, catching us up in hymns of praise and thanksgiving, and placing us alongside those who worked out their relation to God through formulating laws and aphorisms. The text of Scripture is not God's word spoken to us; it reveals God as the one *about* whom, not *by* whom, various types of literature are written. Ricoeur goes further, and sees a providential safeguard of human freedom in precisely this diversity and lack of codification which 'overthrow[s] every totalitarian form of authority which might claim [the right] to withhold the revealed truth . . . the God who reveals himself is a hidden God . . . revelation can never constitute a body of truths which an institution may boast of or take pride in possessing'.[5]

There is a striking anticipation of the distinctions of genre that are essential if we are to avoid assimilating the whole of Scripture to the prophetic, prescriptive paradigm in Richard Hooker – whose doctrine of scriptural authority is indeed in many ways richly nuanced. Writing in some exasperation of opponents who would not accept any ordering of the Church for which they could not find what they regarded as certain warrants in the Bible, Hooker objected that this falsifies Scripture by treating it all as if it were *law*, and ignoring what we would now call differences of genre. The passage is in many ways so modern in tone that I will quote it in full:

> True it is concerning the word of God, whether it be by mis-construction of the sense or by falsification of the words, wit-tingly to endeavour that any thing may seem divine which is not, or any thing not seem which is, were plainly to abuse, and even to falsify divine evidence; which injury offered but unto men, is most worthily counted heinous. Which point I wish they did well observe, with whom nothing is more familiar than to plead in these causes, 'the law of God', 'the word of the Lord', who notwithstanding when they come to allege what word and what law they mean, their common ordinary practice is to quote by-speeches in some historical narration or other, and to urge them as if they were written in most exact form of law. What is to add to the law of God if this be not? When that which the word of God doth but deliver historically, we con-strue without any warrant as if it were legally meant, and so urge it further than we can prove it was intended; do we not add to the laws of God, and make them in number seem more than they are?[6]

That one should not quote 'by-speeches in some historical narra-tion or other' as if they had legal force was a radical and even dangerous doctrine in Hooker's day, and still more in the next century, when the justification of the monarchy out of the books of Kings would become central to much Anglican polemic. (Lancelot Andrewes, for example, would candidly justify the practice of seeking Old Testament passages on which to model the British monarchy by saying 'we have to take our example from the Old Testament, seeing that there is none for us in the New'.[7]) 'Some historical narration or other' in any case hardly sounds like a respectful way of referring to the historical books of the Bible. But in this as in many things Hooker saw more clearly than both his predecessors and his successors. Scripture contains a variety of genres, and to apply historical narration or the speeches of characters in a historical narration as if they stood under the prophetic 'Thus says the Lord' is, as we should say, a category mistake.

Does it follow, therefore, that the Bible has authority for Chris-tians only in those places where there *is* direct appeal to God as the giver of particular rulings or oracles? If by authority we meant legal authority, that might be so. But, as we have seen, the authority of Scripture for Christians is of a much more complex and subtle character than this. The formula 'This is the Word of the Lord', if taken really seriously, ought to make us restrict to a minimum the number of passages to be read liturgically, for fear that it will encourage the kind of mistaken assumption of instant applicability as a divine oracle that Hooker was trying to discourage. But in reality that is not how biblical authority operates in any case, and we may be grateful to the liturgists for having forced us to take note of this by introducing such a dreadful formula – though they may feel this is something of a backhanded compliment.

Apart from the epistles, the teaching material in the Gospels, and some of the Old Testament wisdom literature, most of the Bible is not didactic in form at all. We might suspect, therefore, that the understanding of scriptural readings as some kind of instruction is a complete mistake, a false trail in Christian understanding of Scripture. Liturgical lections are not *lessons* in the ordinary modern sense of that word, but readings: a more neutral term. There are at least two other functions that the Bible discharges when read in public worship, either of which seems to me more central than that of teaching the congregation. We may call them *kerygmatic* and *doxological* functions.[8] The Bible is not read in worship merely to instruct the congregation: it is also read to proclaim the gospel, and as a vehicle by which thanks and praise can be offered to God for what he is and what he has done. Both these functions enable us to move further away than does the didactic function from an over-identification of the Bible with the 'Word of God'. In this way we can do more justice to its character as human words: a classic but not an infallible expression of human response to God, which is read publicly not to inform so much as to inspire and to express praise and celebration.

To speak of the kerygmatic or proclamatory function of Scripture in liturgy is perhaps not to make much more than the familiar point that the Bible is a vehicle for the Word of God rather than simply identical with it. God's Word is communicated, that is, God is able to reach and touch the mind and heart, *through* the reading and exposition of Scripture, but the words of Scripture are not themselves the sum total of his Word. The function of the 'liturgy of the Word' in public worship is not primarily to inform the congregation of the contents and meaning of a particular passage of Scripture, but to proclaim and celebrate God's Word – which is to say, God's input into the human situation. The Church's teaching and the contents of Scripture bear witness to this Word in different ways, and more or less imperfectly.

The difference between didactic and kerygmatic reading can be easily seen if we consider how differently we feel about hearing the St Matthew Passion read every year in Holy Week, and hearing even a particularly good sermon preached for the second time. This is not just a matter of quality, not just that the passion narrative bears frequent repetition: it is a difference of function. People do not arrive at church late on Palm Sunday on the grounds that they already know the story and can afford to miss the reading of it. The gospel is proclaimed in the liturgy, not merely read – as liturgical practices surrounding the book in which it is written bear out, in churches across the whole spectrum of Christian Communions. 'With us', wrote Hooker, 'the reading of Scripture in the church is a part of our church liturgy, a special portion of the service which we do to God.'[9] But this is not a perception peculiar to Anglicans; Catholic, Orthodox, Lutheran, and Reformed Christians might all say the same, though with differing nuances.[10]

The paradigm case for the doxological use of the Bible is of course the Psalms. It is quite unnatural to understand the singing of the Psalms as an example of the Church listening to the Word of God: on the contrary, the Church is manifestly uttering human words to God. And very much of the Church's worship takes the form of reading the Bible or reciting summaries of its central narrative (for example, in the prefaces to eucharistic prayers) which similarly have the character not of divine communication to man, but of human praise offered to God. In this praise the Church recounts to him the things he has done – in a form manifestly shaped by human understanding and human perception. Very rarely, as I have repeatedly stressed, does the Bible itself declare that its narratives about the 'mighty acts of God' are given by God himself as his Word. Normally they are a human account of how God and his works look from a human point of view. When such accounts are read or summarized in public worship, what occurs is not divine teaching, but human praise. Much of the Bible, read in this way, becomes hymn-like, as anyone who has heard (for example) Genesis 1 read at the Easter Vigil can testify. In it we present to God our own best efforts at understanding and expressing his character and give him thanks and praise for his works, as (in George Herbert's expression) 'the secretary of God's praise'.[11] Once we have seen this, we can return to the place of the Bible in liturgy and find, strangely enough, that it is here above all that Ricoeur's insight into the multiple genres in Scripture can be most fruitfully appreciated.

II

It may be said, however, that to locate the authority of the different genres in the Bible in liturgy is to dodge the question why it is these books rather than any others that are in fact used liturgically. Does this not reduce the authority of the Bible beyond what is tolerable, for could we not use absolutely any words in this way? Well, in a sense we could. There are liturgical texts of such antiquity, dignity and importance that they could reasonably be called 'canonical' for the Christian communities that use them. For example, in the Catholic and Lutheran Churches, and increasingly in the Anglican Communion, the Exultet, sung at the Paschal Vigil, has a sort of 'scriptural' status and, notoriously, some of its theology has caused problems for people in those Communions precisely *because* it is quasi-canonical. 'O happy fault, O necessary sin of Adam' resonates through much Western thinking about the problems of theodicy. Perhaps St John Chrysostom's Easter homily has a comparable place in the Greek and Russian Orthodox Churches, and of course for the Orthodox many ancient liturgical texts are more or less 'scriptural'.

Our rather relaxed attitude to the canon means that none of this is a problem. Ultimate authority lies behind and before the Bible, in the 'canon of truth', in the essential *res scripturae* (in Luther's expression[12]), the 'matter' of Scripture, which is communicated when Scripture is read, heard and preached. Nevertheless it is not the case that simply any text can serve as the vehicle for the kinds of kerygmatic and doxological proclamation we have been describing. To return to a theme from the earlier chapters: the only thing that can become new and fresh in the liturgical celebration of the Church (as in its faith) is that which is old, the classic texts which resonate in sympathy with the Church's modern concerns and are forged into a new kind of unity and synthesis in the process.

Perhaps it is here that we can return to Austin Farrer's theology of images,[13] for it is probably in the liturgical sphere more than any other that his insights find their strongest confirmation. In compiling a liturgy, Christians are doing something like what the structural anthropologists call *bricolage*: taking something from here, something from there – materials that lie to hand in the tradition – and forging them into a new unity in which all harmonize as if they had been designed for the purpose.

In a great liturgical celebration — let us again take the Easter Vigil – elements from different times and contexts are blended together in such a way that they come to seem contemporary with each other and, indeed, contemporary with ourselves. As a matter of history we know that the first reading, Genesis 1, comes from (maybe) the fifth century BC, the epistle from the 50s AD, the paschal proclamation from the sixth century AD, parts of the prayers and litanies from the late Middle Ages, and perhaps some of the hymns that are sung from the nineteenth century or even from our own time. But within the liturgy these texts are all perceived as existing in the same time, and as communicating directly with the modern worshipper. Here, again, hermeneutical insight is the contemplation of something that against expectations works and is fruitful, rather than dismayed reflection on a problem that we cannot solve. And it is probably primarily at the level of the great images which unite biblical texts with modern Christian faith that the synthesis is accomplished: water, light, fire, deliverance, freedom. In liturgy we see that using texts and pictures from many different eras and cultures is not a problem but a perfectly normal part of human life, rather like living in a house built over a long time, with rooms and wings of different periods.

Of course this can be far too easily and blandly achieved. The liturgical context can simply collapse the past into the present, assuming continuities between past and present and ignoring discontinuities, and turning the words of the Bible and other ancient texts into merely a vehicle for entirely modern thoughts and perceptions. Elsewhere I have described what happens when old words are simply made a peg on which to hang new meanings as 'creative transcription'[14] – a process which produces what is in fact a new text that simply happens to be verbally identical with an old one. Sometimes, of course, this is no more than an excuse for 'overexegesis', and the transcription is not so much creative of a new text as destructive of the old one. But classic liturgy is not half so naive. In good liturgy we can arrive at something like Steiner's fourth hermeneutic move,[15] in which the old text is both fully appropriated in the present and at the same time fully restored to its original context.

People who live in houses which have grown over the centuries may, indeed, completely lack any historical sense and be simply uncomprehending about the original design of the different parts. But they may also, through their very delight in the harmonious whole that the disparate parts have become, grow to value the parts, explore the historical setting that gave birth to each, and become local historians. Good liturgy invites us all to become local historians of our Christian heritage, and critical historians at that. There is plenty of bad liturgy, plenty of complacent and uncritical use of the Bible, plenty that goes on in our churches to make the critical theologian despair. But liturgy is not really the natural ally of the obscurantist. That is to misunderstand it as inherently what it sometimes becomes in practice, a self-indulgent repetition of meaningless rituals. Good liturgy is the natural ally of a hermeneutic that is alive both to the original sense of texts and to the modern context in which they are being appropriated, and can fuse the two creatively. Good liturgy does not merely comfort, but also hurts, intellectually, emotionally and spiritually.

III

Once again, and now for the last time, our argument has taken the form of a raid on enemy supplies. 'The Bible as literature', as we have seen, has become one of the favourite ploys of conservative biblicism in its never-ceasing quest for some technique to exorcize the spirit of criticism. In much the same way the liturgical use of the Bible is all too often the last refuge of various fundamentalisms – especially perhaps of a Catholic rather than an evangelical kind; though evangelicals too can use the words of Scripture in public worship in a declamatory way that seems to challenge us to examine them critically if we dare.

But the ploy miscarries. Liturgical use of the Bible makes sense only if the Bible is not a series of divine instructions, as on the prophetic paradigm, but contains a variety of genres as wide as the differing liturgical uses to which we put it – narration, praise, petition, confession, and the rest. A thoughtful consideration of the way the Bible functions in worship makes 'This is the Word of the Lord' little more than comic as a concluding formula. But not only so; the apparent timelessness of liturgy, within which critical questions can so easily be dodged, is also an illusion. If we once start to reflect on what we are doing by using old texts, especially though not exclusively the Bible, in public worship, we shall see that we are constantly challenged by it to hold our own experience and the ancient text together, and to do justice to both. To deny this, and to say that the usefulness of the Bible for liturgical practice means that we need never ask critical questions about it, is rather like suggesting that performing Shakespeare is a sovereign remedy against Shakespeare criticism. Shakespeare *can* indeed be performed in such a way that his distance from us is simply annihilated, and all critical questioning is forcibly blocked. At the opposite extreme, of course, he can be performed so 'authentically' that he is totally incomprehensible. But the interesting cases lie in between, or rather, when authenticity and modernity are fused: when the performance is so authentic that it is also modern, so modern that it is also authentic. And the audience at such a performance is not lulled into complacency, but electrified by a charge that leaps the centuries, and leaves the theatre buzzing with questions, alert and full of wonder.

Notes

1. cf. above, pp. 45–6.

2. P. Ricoeur, 'Toward a Hermeneutic of the Idea of Revelation', in his *Essays on Biblical Interpretation*, L. S. Mudge, ed. (Philadelphia 1980, London 1981), pp. 73–118.

3. ibid., p. 76.

4. ibid., p. 91.

5. ibid., p. 95.

6. Richard Hooker, *Of the Laws of Ecclesiastical Polity*, iii.5.

7. Cited in H. Graf Reventlow, *The Authority of Scripture and the Rise of the Modern World* (London 1984), p. 139, from Lancelot Andrewes, *Tortura Torti sive ad Matthaei Torti librum responsio*, *Works* vii (London 1854), p. 446. Cranmer, in his sermon at the coronation of Edward VI in 1547, was already treading this path, calling the young king a new Josiah, who would purify Church and State: see F. L. Baumer, *The Early Tudor Theory of Kingship*, London 1940, and Reventlow, *Authority of Scripture*, p. 109. The British Coronation Service retains strong features of this tradition.

8. cf. my comments in *Believing in the Church: the Corporate Nature of Faith. A Report by the Doctrine Commission of the Church of England* (London 1981), pp. 97–9.

9. Hooker, *Of the Laws of Ecclesiastical Polity*, v. 19.5.

10. cf. A. Schmemann, *The World as Sacrament* (London 1966), pp. 37–8.

11. George Herbert, 'Providence'. See the illuminating discussion in D. W. Hardy and D. F. Ford, *Jubilate: Theology in Praise* (London 1984), pp. 81–2.

12. See Luther, *de servo arbitrio*, 606–9, in A. N. Marlow and B. Drewery, ed., *Luther and Erasmus: Free Will and Salvation*, Library of Christian Classics 17 (London 1959), pp. 109–12, discussed more fully below, pp. 84–6.

13. See above, pp. 36–8.

14. See my *Reading the Old Testament: Method in Biblical Study* (Philadelphia and London 1984), pp. 174–9 and p. 233 note 18.

15. See above, p. 63.

CHAPTER 8

The Word of God and the Words of Men

'The Word was made flesh'

Those unacquainted with the ways of theologians are sometimes surprised at how little one can really discover about their beliefs by inspecting a list of the theological propositions to which they are prepared to assent. This is one reason why the clamour in the Church of England in the last few years for bishops and professors to be forced to make public declarations of a credal kind is so pointless, as well as so pernicious. The bishops' little booklet *The Nature of Christian Belief,*[1] a (mercifully) somewhat half-hearted response to these demands, showed only too clearly that it is always possible to produce a formula which all will accept. This is because people all produce their own exegesis of it so as to accommodate what they really believe within its terms. Anglicans have been doing this since the first promulgation of the Thirty-Nine Articles. The Royal Declaration later prefixed to the Articles tried to put a stop to it, by directing that 'no man hereafter shall either print, or preach, to draw the Article aside any way, but shall submit to it in the plain and full meaning thereof: and shall not put his own sense or comment to be the meaning of the Article, but shall take it in the literal and grammatical sense'. Those who drafted this clause were the lineal descendants of the advisers of King Canute.

But quite apart from the casuistry and deviousness to which Anglicans are perhaps peculiarly prone, there is a more general point here. No list-like statement of Christian belief ever does justice to what Christians believe anyway; for what a list cannot do is to identify the centre of the faith that a person holds, so as to show where the heart of it beats, and how the blood flows out into the other parts of the whole body of belief. One reason, perhaps, why creeds are both so convenient as ecumenical summaries of the faith and yet so uninformative about the realities of Christian belief and practice 'on the ground' is their list-like character. This has two aspects.

First, it makes all the difference in the world which of the items in the creed people make the centre of their living faith. For some this may be a conviction of the fatherhood and creatorship of

God, a Christological claim, belief centred on the Holy Spirit, an attachment to the catholicity of the Church, or a concern for the resurrection of the dead, to name but a few possibilities. But, secondly, there are others who would claim to give equal weight to all the articles of the creed, but insist that it has value only within some overarching principle by which Christian faith is organized. Lutherans, for example, repeat the creed in public worship nearly as much as Catholics and Anglicans; but they will want to insist that the creed is abused unless it is understood as part of the gospel, that is, as proclaiming good news about the grace of God towards mankind. If it is treated as a checklist of what God requires us to believe before he will bless us, it is being made into an instrument of the law, not of the gospel. That is a wholly different understanding of the creed from the one held, for example, by those who press the General Synod to compel bishops to declare their credal faith. The fact that both sorts of Christians use and value the creed is deeply uninformative about the styles of religion of such widely different types of person.

I

In this chapter I must sum up the argument of this book about the Bible as a source of authority for Christian faith. I find myself faced with ostensible agreements among Christian theologians which nevertheless conceal vast divergences, precisely because they do not even hint at the different ways in which the Bible functions in the concrete practice of the Christian faith. There are two propositions that at any rate all Protestant theology agrees on, which in opposite ways exemplify this slipperiness of religious language. The first is this: that it is not primarily the Bible that is the Word of God, but Jesus Christ. I do not think one could find a single Christian who would dissent from this proposition, for to do so would plainly be to commit what is sometimes called bibliolatry: the elevation of the Bible above Christ himself. In making so much of this very theme, therefore, have we not ourselves been guilty of shying at straw men? Certainly not; for it is one thing to accept the formal principle that God speaks through Christ primarily rather than through the Bible, and quite another to allow this principle actually to make a difference to the way we handle the Bible in our daily practice of the Christian faith, or in theological reflection on it.

Karl Barth, for example, stated the principle most clearly: the Bible is not, simply and literally, the Word of God. The Word of God is the One who was in the beginning with God, that is, Christ. The Bible and the word of preaching by which Christ is proclaimed are both called the Word of God by a transfer from him, secondarily and as it were metaphorically. Both of them *become* God's Word, God's communication of himself into the human situation, when they are read or heard in faith, when Christ is present to the believer; under such circumstances and not otherwise they participate in that function of mediating God to man which belongs properly only to Jesus Christ himself.

> The Bible is . . . not itself and in itself God's past revelation, just as Church proclamation also is not itself and in itself the expected future revelation . . . The Bible witnesses point beyond themselves . . . Why and in what respect does the Biblical witness possess authority? In that it claims no authority whatever for itself, that its witness amounts to letting the something else be the authority, itself and by its own agency. Therefore we do the Bible a poor honour, and one unwelcome to itself, when we directly identify it with this something else, with revelation itself.[2]

All this is truly and rightly said. But does it make any difference in practice to what people who revere Barth do with the Bible; does it make them any less prone to effective bibliolatry? It does not. The proposition that Christ, and not the Bible, is the true Word of God is not at the living heart of the religion of most of those deeply influenced by Neo-orthodox theology. Rather, it is a kind of concessive clause, a necessary safeguard at the borders of faith, designed to prevent actual heresy. It is undeniably accurate as a statement of the theoretical limits of the Christian faith, but not an important central doctrine. For practical purposes, the careful theological qualifications can be ignored; for living the Christian life from day to day we shall, if we are Christians of a Neo-orthodox turn of mind, treat the Bible as the Word of God without qualification and rely on it as an infallible and inerrant source of doctrine and ethical guidance. Thus the proposition that only Christ is properly the Word of God will not be denied, but it will not make any practical difference to our faith.

One major purpose of this book has been to try to move Barth's recognition that only Christ is truly the Word of God into the centre of attention. What would be the result of taking it seriously, not as a last-ditch safeguard against some heresy that might be seen more as a theoretical than a practical danger, but as an essential and central insight into the nature of authority for the Christian? For bibliolatry is not a merely theoretical danger: it is a daily reality in the modern Church. We cannot afford to note Barth's careful distinction, but then pass on, continuing to treat the Bible as if it were really identical with Jesus Christ. We need to use our commitment to Christ as a living instrument with which to make the subordinate position of the Bible a reality.

Christians are not those who believe in the Bible, but those who believe in Christ. It should by now be more than clear that I do not believe there is any practical way to Christ today that does not involve the Bible at some point on the road. I am quite sure the authenticity of our knowledge of and faith in Christ cannot be established unless we have the Bible, the earliest documents of the Christian religion, to act as a check and a source. Equally, the truth that the Bible can indeed become the Word of God, God's way of continuing to speak to the Church, when it is heard and read in faith, is for me beyond dispute. But all this is a million miles away from enthroning the Bible as the sole arbiter of what is Christian, in faith or practice; binding the Church to so-called 'scriptural' doctrines; requiring other sources of knowledge to be rejected in the name of scriptural authority; and – the ultimate contradiction – forcing the Bible to say what we want to hear, because we cannot believe anything unless we think it is from the Bible that we are hearing it. This is to press a valuable metaphor – the Bible as God's Word – as though it were a literal definition of ultimate truth, and indeed the most important and central such definition in the Christian faith.

Here, then, is a case where something which is consistently affirmed by all has not been allowed to become truly functional for faith. But it needs to become so if Christians are not to become a 'people of the book' in a sense inimical to the gospel of free redemption in Christ. But at the same time as modern Protestantism has failed to take seriously one proposition about the Bible which all theoretically agree on, it has pressed in a most literal way another proposition which really does originate as a boundary-marker rather than as a central and positive theological definition. This is the insistence, clear in all the Reformers, that it is Scripture rather than tradition that must be the arbiter in matters of faith. Against the Catholic position, the insistence on *sola scriptura* is meant to prevent the indefinite development of Christianity into an ever-changing religion, where in fact 'Christianity' means simply 'what the Church happens now to believe'.[3] It insists that there is unchanging evidence for what the Christian faith originally was, against which later developments can be checked for authenticity. Furthermore, Scripture 'is its own interpreter'. That is, we may not smuggle back in through the back door what we have just expelled at the front by saying that, although indeed Scripture alone has authority, yet it is to the Church – and hence to ongoing ecclesiastical tradition – that we have to look if we want to find out what Scripture means.

All this is consistent with the idea of the canon of Scripture in its primary and original sense: a *maximum* list, a negative and limiting standard, which says, Thus far and no further. In this sense the canonization of Scripture (that is, its *limitation* to particular books) is not a hermeneutical or any other kind of positive evaluation of Scripture, but a negative one. It says that nothing has the authority of the gospel if it cannot be found here. It does *not* say that what is found here is a perfect or uniquely profound expression of the gospel, only that this is the norm against which other expressions are to be judged.

Now surely here we have the equal and opposite problem from that presented a few moments ago. In Protestant theology since the Reformation the principle of *sola scriptura* has been far from this essentially minimal and limiting principle. It has become the basis for all sorts of maximalizing claims about the Bible.

Perhaps we may put the matter like this. The true character of the opposition between gospel or Scripture and subsequent tradition, which is a qualitative one, has come to be misunderstood as quantitative. For Luther, say, Scripture was different in kind from subsequent tradition, because it was to be seen as the primary witness to the gospel in its original form. It did not function as tradition had come to function, as the horizon within which all Christian thinking had to take place, but as something objective, set over against the Church and demanding that its hard edges be respected.

But in subsequent Protestant orthodoxy, the Bible began to function in exactly the same way as ecclesiastical tradition functions for Catholics, except that it was a tradition that had been artificially truncated. Scripture, for most sorts of Protestantism, is simply Catholic tradition with all the bits that happen not to lie within the pages of the Bible artificially removed. Because this tradition thus does not reach down to us, but is as it were unnaturally foreshortened, complicated hermeneutical procedures are needed – as they are not in Catholicism – to enable it to continue to speak to us, and to make it *feel* like the tradition within which we stand. The result is more or less artificial readings of the text. But this radically falsifies the original Reformation insight into the status of Scripture as something which *ought* to feel somewhat alien and set over against us.

II

It may be possible to illustrate this from one of the most famous Reformation debates, that between Luther and Erasmus about the question of the clarity or perspicuity of Scripture. This is the debate that produced Luther's *de servo arbitrio*, 'On the Bondage of the Will', written in 1525.[4] The introductory material contains Luther's objections to Erasmus' argument that the Bible contains many obscurities, and consequently needs to be expounded by the authoritative magisterium of the Church if it is to exercise any authority over Christians.

On the face of it, Erasmus was of course in the right in maintaining that the Bible had obscurities. If it is to be the primary authority for Christian faith, we need alongside the text an equally authoritative tradition of interpretation which will illuminate them. A uniquely authoritative text of no determinable meaning could only be the gift of a somewhat sardonic, Cartesian deity, not of the God and Father of our Lord Jesus Christ. As usual in theological debates, however, the protagonists were at cross purposes. When Luther insists against Erasmus that the Bible is *not* obscure or dark but plain and clear, it is important to notice that he does not mean by 'the Bible' or 'Scripture' exactly what Erasmus meant: this long and complex text, with so many obviously obscure passages. Indeed, he does not precisely say that 'Scripture' is clear. He says that the *res scripturae*, the 'matter' of Scripture, is clear, and he glosses this as follows:

> What kind of deep secret can still be hidden in the Scripture, now that the seals have been opened, the stone rolled away from the grave, and the deepest secret of all revealed: that Christ, the only Son of God, has become man, that there is one eternal God in three persons, that Christ has died for us, and that he reigns for ever in heaven?[5]

What is clear, we may say, is not exactly 'Scripture' but 'the gospel' – 'the rule of faith', as we may recall it was sometimes called in the early Church.

Luther's polemic is not really directed against the idea that some places in the Bible are difficult to interpret, but against the idea that it is in biblical interpretation – and hence through a hermeneutical tradition, watched over by the *ecclesia docens* – that Christian truth is made known. On the contrary, he argues, the Christian gospel has been made plain by God himself, it does not lie encoded in a book. This gospel exists before and apart from any instantiation in the words of the text. Indeed, the text can itself be tested against the gospel. Consistently with this, Luther himself – unlike most of his followers – was willing to criticize books in the canon. For him, *books* of Scripture are not the heart of God's Word anyway. Books are a second best to the oral proclamation of the gospel.

There is a place in the Sherlock Holmes story *Silver Blaze* which has passed into legend, where Holmes draws Watson's attention to 'the curious incident of the dog in the night-time'. The dog in question did nothing in the night-time; that was the curious incident.[6] In a similar vein, we might draw attention to the curious case of Luther's treatise *de sacra scriptura*. What is curious about it, of course, is that it does not exist. Unlike Calvin, Luther never devoted a lengthy work to the problem of the Bible and its interpretation, as part of the epistemological or hermeneutical prolegomena to systematic theology. The Bible was the air he breathed, but it was not a subject for this kind of treatment. What was crucial was the 'matter' of Scripture: the saving gospel of God's love to sinners, revealed in Christ.

This insight was quickly lost even in Lutheranism, which became just as bibliocentric as other branches of Protestant tradition. But I believe it is essential for us to recapture it. *Sola scriptura* is not and ought not to become the central pillar of anyone's understanding of the Christian faith. *Sola scriptura* is a metaphor. It points us, somewhat epigrammatically, to the truth that the gospel is of God's making, and that human words and traditions cannot contain it. Every attempt to identify this gospel with the words of a book, even of the Bible, is to turn it into human tradition and thereby to domesticate it; and this deprives it of its power to stand over against our own thoughts and ideas and to challenge us to revise them. In turning *sola scriptura* from a symbol by which the God-given character of the gospel is defended into a literal and positive statement about where its heart can be found, the Protestant Churches sold their birthright for a mess of hermeneutics. In its emphasis on Scripture as against tradition, Protestants had a potent symbol of the primacy of God's input over human appropriation of it;[7] but they flattened the symbol through a wooden literalness, and so merely replaced one kind of human tradition with another, a human Pope with a paper Pope.

Protestant orthodoxy, in its very determination to find in the Bible a source of authority which could be opposed to the authority of the Catholic Church, thus took the fateful step of accepting as common ground the need for some authority that could resolve doctrinal disputes definitively and infallibly. It is not so much that the Bible is not the correct candidate for that position, as that the position is not available. The gospel, as Luther saw, is not about the kind of conceptual certainty that either kind of Pope can provide: it is about the encounter with a gracious God. Of course this does not mean an anti-intellectual fideism in which doctrinal formulations are to be eschewed, or an anarchic view of the Church in which no one is ever permitted to rule on disputes;

but it does mean setting one's face resolutely against the all-too-human delusion that someone, somewhere, has all the answers.

III

As I look back over the course of this book I find that I have been attempting two tasks, which have run in parallel. I have not been concerned to counter in any systematic way what I think are false views of biblical authority; the principal modern distortion, as I see it, is fundamentalism, and others have marshalled all the arguments against that long before me. Nevertheless, the discussion has involved a good deal of engagement with fundamentalism and with other, more subtle, pleas for the Bible to be immune from the kind of biblical criticism which is my daily work. I have tried to meet these movements by the kind of *ad hominem* argument that may be called spoiling the Egyptians: taking the best arguments one's opponents have to offer, and turning them to one's own use. I have tried to grant all that may be granted to the fundamentalists' case, but then to show that their most precious jewels shine more brightly in a setting provided by critical theology than in the one they were designed for.

In chapter 1 we examined the argument that a high doctrine of scriptural authority is part of the heritage we have received from the earliest Christians by asking how, then, Scripture was understood by St Paul and by Jesus himself. In place of the simple biblicism that might have been expected, we found a complex mixture of an extreme reverence for the Jewish Scriptures and an extreme freedom from them. Probing beneath the surface of this complexity, we saw it resting on a commitment to a faith which was both new and old, which claimed that the God who was truly revealed in the old Scriptures had none the less done something new, which could not be contained within the constraints they imposed. The ambiguity in which this involved the Old Testament in particular is accordingly not a modern invention, produced by woolly liberalism, but an inherent and irreducible part of the Christian gospel from the beginning.

It is tempting to say, however, that Christians soon resolved the ambiguity, or at least stabilized it, by devising a Bible made up of 'Old' and 'New' Testaments. The relation of the two parts was formally defined according to the scheme 'promise and fulfilment'. But again, as we saw in chapter 2, a return to the earliest sources yields nothing like such a tidy picture. This neat hermeneutical scheme is only a fragment of the earliest Christian understanding of Scripture. Early Christians applied it only informally and occasionally, and if we are to appeal to them for support, we shall have to accept something far more untidy than we might like. Anyone, therefore, who raises the ghost of the appeal to messianic prophecy in order to answer the question of the authority of the Bible must expect to find that other spirits come up with it; and some of them are more kindly disposed to so-called liberals than to conservative biblicism.

Among these spirits is one which points to the reality of God's self-disclosure in Judaism; and another reminds us that the very identity of the Scriptures, both 'Old' and 'New', was by no means agreed or even discussed in the earliest days of the Church. The *canon* in fact concerned us in chapter 3, and here again there was scope for an outflanking manoeuvre. We tried to show that when the early Fathers spoke of a 'canon' they meant a rule of faith, by which even the contents of Scripture could be judged, rather than an immutable list of holy books. The strong sense of the canon as a kind of single coherent work, which has become popular in modern theology, was in any case unknown in earlier times. If we are to make theological use of this *modern* idea of a canon – an idea which has had a fruitful career in secular literary criticism – it will be more naturally applied by analogy to precisely the ambiguous relation of old to new in the Christian faith that makes the notion of a codified sacred document with hard edges so difficult to accept. If, therefore, you would like a 'canonical' account of the Christian faith in this pregnant, modern sense of the word 'canonical', you can have one, but much more easily by abandoning biblicism than by holding on to it.

Perhaps in subsequent chapters the prevalence of this style of argument was more obvious, and needs less elaboration here. In chapter 4 we tried to show that the evidential value of the Bible, as well as its theological content, will have freer scope if we understand the Bible as something which we are allowed to dig beneath than if it is treated, on the conservative model, as encapsulated in its own sacred world. In chapter 5 we saw that the successful attempt in modern times to treat it as a finished 'text' with literary and religious power as it stands can be satisfactorily explained only if our general hermeneutical theory encourages us to distance it, and to value its historical particularity. Finally, in chapter 7, we argued that even the liturgical use of Scripture is a better ally in the cause of a critical than of a biblicist programme. The kind of liturgy that removes liturgically used texts from critical enquiry is an escapist liturgy, and hardly the kind of thing thoughtful biblicists could be happy with as a support for their case.

So much for one thread of argument that has run through our discussion. I do seriously believe that many conservative positions, if thought through consistently, point in the very opposite direction from the one in which their proponents are trying to lead us. I think, in fact, that they frequently score own goals; and while I have sympathy for this tendency, since I have never in my life scored any other kind, I haven't been able to resist the desire to blow the whistle. But I hope that the argument has not all been *ad hominem*, but that some positive lines of thought have emerged and can take their chance outside a polemical context. Central to my own thinking about the authority of the Bible is the conviction that we can say nothing worthwhile about the Bible except by beginning with the Christian gospel that existed before there ever was a Bible and could survive if every Bible was destroyed. The centre of the gospel is not about knowledge, but about love: the love of God for a fallen world, and his will to restore it through Christ. About this gospel the Bible – in both Testaments – provides us with all kinds of information, both historical and theological. By reading the Bible, studying it with all our critical powers, using it in worship, and being challenged by it as a literary text, we can come face to face with the gospel and respond to it with our whole lives. If that is not to accord authority to the Bible, I do not know what would be.

If we start at the centre, with the gospel of Christ, we shall have no difficulty at all in discovering how indispensable the Bible is. But theories of biblical authority do not, it seems to me, commonly start at the centre. They are more often than not theologies of the limiting case, arising from such questions as: What is the ultimate court of appeal for deciding matters of doctrine? At what point did Christian writings cease to be inspired? Precisely which words represent the authoritative text of Scripture? How can every single word of the Bible be applied to the circumstances of the present day? How can we show that Scripture contains no loose ends? What is the irreducible minimum (or, alternatively, the absolute maximum) of doctrine or ethics that is binding on or permissible for Christians? It is of course conceivable that God intends us to be able to give definitive answers to such questions; but if so, then Catholics must be right to maintain that he needs to provide some *human* authority to whom we can turn, for Protestants are certainly wrong if they think that the Bible can answer them. What kind of providence, intending to produce an authoritative code of that kind, would have given us the Bible?

But if what we need is not a source of rulings, but access to (again in Luther's great phrase) the matter of Scripture, the gospel of the love of God, then the Bible will do well enough – just as the Church will do well enough, and all human institutions and inventions that respond to God with faltering and imperfect voices will do well enough. In religion especially, the best is often the enemy of the good, and we cannot see the good fortune we have for crying after a perfection that is impossible to anything human. Let us leave the last word to Richard Hooker:

> Whatsoever is spoken of God, or things appertaining to God, otherwise than as the truth is, though it seem an honour, it is an injury. And as incredible praises given unto men do often abate and impair the credit of their deserved commendation; so we must likewise take great heed, lest, in attributing unto Scripture more than it can have, the incredibility of that do cause even those things which indeed it hath most abundantly, to be less reverently esteemed.[8]

Notes

1. *The Nature of Christian Belief: A Statement and Exposition by the House of Bishops of the General Synod of the Church of England*, London 1986.

2. K. Barth, *Church Dogmatics* I/1 (Edinburgh 1975), pp. 125–6.

3. cf. A. T. Hanson, *The New Testament Interpretation of Scripture* (London 1980), p. 19, commenting on both Catholic and Protestant forms of the belief that 'Christianity is just what it happens to be at any time or place'.

4. For the texts, see *Luther and Erasmus: Free Will and Salvation*, Library of Christian Classics 17, London 1959. The volume has an introduction by A. N. Marlow and B. Drewery (pp. 1–32). Detailed discussions of the perspicuity of Scripture in Luther may be found in F. Beisser, *Claritas Scripturae bei Martin Luther*, Forschungen zur Kirchen- und Dogmengeschichte 18, Göttingen 1966, and O. Kuss, 'Über die Klarheit der Schrift: historische und hermeneutische Überlegungen zu der Kontroverse des Erasmus und des Luther über den freien oder versklavten Willen', in *Theologie und Glaube* 60 (1970), pp. 273–321, reprinted in J. Ernst, ed., *Schriftauslegung. Beiträge zur Hermeneutik des Neuen Testaments und im Neuen Testament*, Munich 1972.

5. *.de servo arbitrio* 606, in *Luther and Erasmus: Free Will and Salvation*, p. 110.

6. A. Conan Doyle, 'Silver Blaze', *Strand Magazine* 1892; in *The Memoirs of Sherlock Holmes*, London 1894.

7. cf. M. F. Wiles, 'The Uses of "Holy Scripture"', in M. Hooker and C. Hickling, ed., *What about the New Testament? Essays in Honour of Christopher Evans* (London 1975), pp. 155–64, who outlines the dangers in the existence of a fixed, canonical Scripture but adds: 'Can we be free of such dangers while still holding on to "holy scripture" as a *symbol* of that objectivity, that otherness, that address to us which is at the heart of faith in a personal God?' (p. 160; Wiles' emphasis).

8. Hooker, *Of the Laws of Ecclesiastical Polity*, ii.8.

Select Bibliography

The topics discussed in this book may be studied further in the following works.

Alter, R. and Kermode, F., ed., *The Literary Guide to the Bible*. London: Collins; Cambridge MA: Harvard University Press 1987.

Barr, J., *The Bible in the Modern World*. London: SCM Press; New York: Harper & Row 1973.

Barr, J., *Escaping from Fundamentalism*. London: SCM Press; published in the US as *Beyond Fundamentalism*. Philadelphia: Westminster 1984.

Barr, J., *Holy Scripture: Canon, Authority, Criticism*. Oxford: Oxford University Press; Philadelphia: Westminster 1983.

Barton, J., *Reading the Old Testament: Method in Biblical Study*. London: Darton, Longman and Todd; Philadelphia: Westminster 1984.

Barton, J., *Oracles of God: Perceptions of Ancient Prophecy in Israel after the Exile*. London: Darton, Longman and Todd 1986.

Brown, R. E., *The Critical Meaning of the Bible*. London: Geoffrey Chapman; Ramsey, NJ: Paulist Press 1981.

Bruce, F. F. and Rupp, E. G., ed, *Holy Book and Holy Tradition*. Manchester: Manchester University Press; Grand Rapids MI: Eerdmans 1968.

von Campenhausen, H., *The Formation of the Christian Bible*. London: A. & C. Black 1972.

Dodd, C. H., *The Authority of the Bible*. 1929, reprinted London: Fontana 1960.

Evans, C. F., *Is 'Holy Scripture' Christian? and Other Questions*. London: SCM Press 1971.

Farrer, A. M., *The Glass of Vision*. London: Dacre Press 1948.

Franklin, E., *How the Critics Can Help*. London: SCM Press 1982.

Frei, H. W., *The Eclipse of Biblical Narrative: A Study in Eighteenth and Nineteenth Century Hermeneutics*. New Haven, NY: Yale University Press 1974.

Hodgson, L. et al., *On the Authority of the Bible*. London: SPCK 1960.

Kelsey, D. H., *The Uses of Scripture in Recent Theology*. London: SCM Press; Philadelphia: Fortress Press 1975.

Muddiman, J., *The Bible: Fountain and Well of Truth*. Oxford: Basil Blackwell 1983.

Nineham, D. E., *The Use and Abuse of the Bible*. London: SPCK 1978; New York: Harper & Row 1977.

Reventlow, H. Graf, *The Authority of the Bible and the Rise of the Modern World*. London: SCM Press; Philadelphia: Fortress Press 1984.

Ricoeur, P., *Essays on Biblical Interpretation*. London: SPCK; Philadelphia: Fortress Press 1981.

Stuhlmacher, P., *Historical Criticism and Theological Interpretation of Scripture*. London: SPCK 1979; Philadelphia: Fortress Press 1977.

Sundberg, A. C., 'Canon of the NT', *Interpreter's Dictionary of the Bible* Supplementary Volume (Nashville, Tenn.: Abingdon 1976), pp. 136–40.

Theissen, G., *Biblical Faith: an Evolutionary Approach*. London: SCM Press; Philadelphia: Fortress Press 1985.

Theissen, G., *On Having a Critical Faith*. London: SCM Press 1979.

Index

Abraham 28, 35
Abraham, W. J. 46
Acts, Book of 14, 18, 41, 70, 71
Adam 26, 34
Agag 71
agrapha 30, 39
Alter, R. 58, 69, 91
Andrewes, Lancelot 73
Augustine 13

Bampton Lectures 36, 56
Barnabas, Epistle of 4, 15–16, 22, 26
Barr, J. x, 10, 11, 22, 24, 33–4, 35, 42, 46, 47, 49, 58, 69, 91
Barth, K. 23, 47, 81–2, 90
Barton, J. 34, 35, 68, 69, 77, 79, 91
Bates, E. S. 68
Baumgartner, W. 23
Beisser, F. 90
Berkhof, H. 22
bibliolatry 38, 81, 82
Brown, R. E. 91
Bruce, F. F. 91
Bultmann, R. 29, 35
Butler, M. 35

Cain 31
Calvin, Jean 86
von Campenhausen, H. 6, 7, 8, 10, 11, 18, 19, 22, 30, 35, 39, 46, 91

canon 6, 24–35, 53, 60–1, 88
canonical criticism 27–8, 34, 47, 49, 59, 65
Chadwick, H. 35, 46
Childs, B. S. 27, 34, 69
Chrysostom, John 31, 76
church order 4, 70, 79
classic 32–3, 60–1, 66–7, 74
Clement, First Epistle of 4, 19, 26
Clementine Recognitions 16, 22
Cobb, J. B. 69
Conan Doyle, A. 90
Corinthians, First Epistle to 17, 18
Curtis, P. 68

David 14
Dawkins, R. 50, 58
Deutero–Isaiah 14
Didache 44
Dodd, C. H. 45, 47, 58, 91
Drewery, B. 79, 90

Ebeling, G. 64, 69
ecclesia docens 41, 85
Eliot, T. S. 32–3, 35
Enoch, First Book of 25
Erasmus, Desiderius 79, 84–6, 90
Ernesti, J. 69
Evans, C. F. 24, 34, 91
Eve 34

Exodus, Book of 26
Ezekiel, Book of 14

Farrer, A. M. 36–8, 44–5, 46, 47, 68, 76, 91
Ford, D. F. 79
Franklin, E. 91
Frei, H. W. 47, 91
Frye, N. 61, 68, 69
Fuchs, E. 69
fundamentalism ix, 1–2, 8, 12, 21, 40, 48, 64–5, 78, 83, 88

Galatians, Epistle to 28
Genesis, Book of 15, 26, 28, 34–5, 75, 76
Gospels, 39–43, 74, 75
Green, G. 22, 46, 47

Hanson, A. T. 90
Hardy, D. W. 79
Harnack, A. von 6, 7, 11
Headlam, A. C. 34
Hebrews, Epistle to 14, 16
Herbert, George 75, 79
hermeneutics 3, 7, 11, 19, 58, 59–69, 77, 88
historical criticism 42–4, 49, 52–3, 54–5, 57
Hodgson, L. 91
Holloway, D. 46
Holmer, P. 35
Holmes, Sherlock 86
Holtzer, S. W. 46
Hooker, Richard 72–5, 79, 90
Houlden, J. L. 46, 60, 68

Ignatius of Antioch 4–5, 6, 10
inerrancy 1, 44, 66, 82
infallibility 44–5, 66, 82, 86–7, 89

inspiration 36–7, 43, 45, 72
Irenaeus 30, 39–40, 43, 46, 53, 54, 58
Isaiah, Book of 13, 19
Islam 1, 34

Jenkins, D. E. 40
Jeremiah, Book of 14
Jezebel 31
John, Gospel of 27, 42, 49
John, Third Epistle of 60
Joshua 15
Jowett, B. 20, 22
Jubilees, Book of 47
Judaism 13–17, 20–2, 63
'judaizing' 5, 17
Jude, Epistle of 25
Judges, Book of 71

Kelsey, D. H. 34, 47, 50, 58, 69, 91
Kermode, F. 58, 61, 69, 91
Kimmerle, H. 69
Kuss, O. 90

Lentricchia, F. 35
Lessing, G. E. 30, 35, 42, 46
liberalism 1–2, 5, 8, 13, 37–8, 59, 88
literary criticism 60–1, 67–8
Lonergan, B. J. F. 46
Louth, A. 10, 47
Luther, Martin 9, 17, 76, 79, 84–6, 89, 90

Marcion 5, 6, 10, 11, 46
Marlow, A. N. 79, 90
Martyrdom of Isaiah 34
Matthew, Gospel of 4, 74–5
Mays J. L. 46

Melito of Sardis, Paschal
    Homily of 10, 11, 26
Michel, O. 6, 11, 22
Mitchell, B. G. 46
Moses 71
Muddiman, J. B. 10, 91

Neo-orthodoxy 82
New Hermeneutic 64, 69
Nahum, Book of 60
Nebuchadnezzar 31
Nicholson, E. W. x
Nineham, D. E. 91
Numbers, Book of 70

O'Donovan, O. M. T. 35
Origen 19, 40, 65, 66

Parker, D. 62
Pastoral Epistles 27
Paul 5, 6, 7, 8, 12, 17, 18, 19, 20,
    21, 25, 26, 28, 29, 41, 53, 70,
    87
Pentateuch 14, 20
perspicuity of Scripture 61,
    84–6
Peter 4, 14
Philip 41
positivism 40–2, 47
prophecy 6, 13–19, 26, 87–8
Psalms 14, 15, 27–8, 71, 75

Qur'an 1, 34

Reformation 5, 17, 43, 54, 64,
    67, 83–7
regula fidei 30–1, 33, 35, 53–5,
    76, 85
revelation 7, 19, 37–8, 40, 55–7,
    60, 71–3
Reventlow, H. Graf 79, 91

Ricoeur, P. 7, 11, 71–2, 75, 79,
    92
Robinson, J. A. T. 55, 58
Robinson, J. M. 69
Rogerson, J. W. 58
Romans, Epistle to 17, 26, 34–5
Rupp, E. G. 91

Samuel 71
Samuel, First Book of 71
Sanday, W. 34
Sauter, G. x
Schleiermacher, F. D. E. 6, 11,
    62, 64, 69
Schmemann, A. 79
Schmidt, W. H. x
semantic indeterminacy 19–20,
    28–9, 61–2, 77
Semler, J. S. 26, 34
Shakespeare, William 66, 78
Smend, R. x, 10, 11, 23
sola scriptura 83–7, 90
Steiner, G. 62–4, 69, 77
Stendahl, K. 47, 69
Strauss, D. F. 42, 46
Stuhlmacher, P. 92
Sundberg, A. C. 35, 92
Synoptic Gospels 5

Teilhard de Chardin, P. 50, 58
Tennyson, Alfred 58
Theissen, G. 50–5, 58, 67, 69, 92
Thiemann, R. 47
Thirty-Nine Articles of
    Religion 24, 35, 80
Thiselton, A. C. 69
Torah 14, 20, 21
tradition 7–8, 27, 33, 41, 76–7,
    84

Waldensians 20
Watson, Dr 86

Wellhausen, J. 57, 58
Wiles, M. F. 19, 22, 47, 56, 58, 90
wisdom literature 45, 56, 71, 74

Wisdom of Solomon 25, 34
Wittgenstein, L. 38
Wood, C. M. 47
worship 3, 30–1, 70–9, 88